# THE STORM WITHIN

## THE DEMONS WE DEAL WITH EVERY DAY

### DR. RONALD LAYBOLT

◆ **FriesenPress**

Suite 300 - 990 Fort St
Victoria, BC, V8V 3K2
Canada

www.friesenpress.com

**Copyright © 2019 by Ronald Laybolt**
First Edition — 2019

All rights reserved.

No part of this publication may be reproduced in any form, or by any means, electronic or mechanical, including photocopying, recording, or any information browsing, storage, or retrieval system, without permission in writing from FriesenPress.

The information on this book is not intended nor implied to be a substitute for professional medical advice, diagnosis or treatment. All content, including text, graphics, images, and information, contained on or available through this book is for general information purposes only.

My Book is not a replacement for professional medical opinion, examination, diagnosis or treatment. Always seek the advice of your medical doctor or another qualified health professional before starting any new treatment or making any changes to existing treatment. Do not delay seeking or disregard medical advice based on information written in this book.

ISBN
978-1-5255-6147-4 (Hardcover)
978-1-5255-6148-1 (Paperback)
978-1-5255-6149-8 (eBook)

1. SELF-HELP, POST-TRAUMATIC STRESS DISORDER (PTSD)

Distributed to the trade by The Ingram Book Company

# DISCLAIMER / LEGAL

The information in this book is not intended or implied to be a substitute for professional medical advice, diagnosis, or treatment. All content, including text, graphics, images, and information contained in or available through this book is for general information purposes only.

My book is not a replacement for professional medical opinion, examination, diagnosis, or treatment. Always seek the advice of your medical doctor or other qualified health professional before starting any new treatment or making any changes to existing treatment. Do not delay seeking or disregard medical advice based on information written in this book. No health questions or information in this book is regulated or evaluated by the Food and Drug Administration, and therefore, the information should not be used to diagnose, treat, cure, or prevent any disease without the supervision of a medical doctor.

# TABLE OF CONTENTS

Disclaimer / Legal ................................................................. iii
Dedication ............................................................................ xi
Introduction to Mental Health ............................................. 1

**Chapter 1: How to Recognize Mental Health** ................. 3
    How Mental Health Relates to Depression ...................... 5
    How Mental Health Affects Family, Friends, and Co-Workers ........... 6
    My Swiss Air Flight 111 - Trauma Never Ends ................. 9
    The Days We Should Not Worry ...................................... 12

**Chapter 2: Post-Traumatic Stress Disorder** ................. 13
    PTSD for Military and First Responders ......................... 14
    Symptoms of Post-Traumatic Stress Disorder and Treatment .......... 17
    Prevention of Post-Traumatic Stress Disorder ................ 18
    Lead by Example .............................................................. 20
    Camp Butmir – The Demons ........................................... 22
    Suffering from Nightmares and Panic Attacks ................ 25
    Trying to Raise a Family with PTSD ................................ 26
    Leaving the Battlefield ..................................................... 28
    My Journey to PTSD and Back ........................................ 31

**Chapter 3: Depression** ................................................... 35
    Signs and Symptoms of Depression ............................... 37
    You're Not Stuck .............................................................. 38

- Why Depression Leads to Self-Harm ... 38
- I am Depression ... 40
- Effects of Self-Harm ... 40
- You Got 'Em ... 41
- The Sad Thing ... 42
- When You Think This is the Last Day ... 43
- I Don't Care ... 44

## Chapter 4: Season Affective Disorder (SAD) ... 45
- Symptoms of SAD ... 46
- Treatment of SAD ... 48
- I Embrace Change ... 48
- Light Therapy for SAD ... 49
- Psychotherapy for SAD ... 50
- Mind-body Connection for SAD ... 50
- History of SAD ... 50
- Lifestyle methods to cope with Seasonal Affective Disorder ... 51
- Living With SAD ... 54
- A Man's SAD Story ... 55

## Chapter 5: Addiction ... 59
- Addiction vs. Misuse ... 61
- My Bout with Addiction ... 61
- Symptoms of Addiction ... 62
- The Top 10 Most Common Addictions ... 63
- Treatments of Addiction ... 64
- The Cost of Addiction ... 65
- Addiction Expenditures ... 66
- Loss of Income and Productivity ... 67
- Bills and Insurance Costs ... 67
- Social Costs ... 67
- Disproportionate Impact on Lower Income Families ... 68

    Physical Complications.................................................68
    Heroin Stole my Life ....................................................70
    The Truth about Life as a Heroin Addict........................ 71
    I Found Myself Taking More and More Pills to Keep Up...................72
    In case you need this today...........................................75
    A Mother's Bouts with Pain ..........................................76

## Chapter 6: Anxiety ................................................................79
    Types of Anxiety Disorders ..........................................80
    Causes and Risk Factors of Anxiety Disorders ............. 81
    Living in Hell .................................................................81
    Signs and Symptoms of Anxiety..................................82
    Diagnosing Anxiety Disorder .......................................83
    Treating Anxiety...........................................................84
    Managing Anxiety Disorder Symptoms........................85
    "I'm here NATO"............................................................86
    When I realized I was struggling with Anxiety..............87
    My Heart was About to Explode ..................................88

## Chapter 7: Dementia ...........................................................91
    Memory Loss and Symptoms of Dementia.................92
    Causes of Dementia ...................................................93
    Diagnosis of Dementia ...............................................94
    Dementia Risk and Prevention....................................94
    Different Categories of Dementia................................96
    Dementia is More than Memory..................................99
    How my Mum Slipped Away ......................................99

## Chapter 8: Sleep Problems ............................................. 103
    Insomnia ...................................................................104
    Sleep Apnea ..............................................................107
    Restless Legs Syndrome (RLS)..................................109

Narcolepsy ........................................................................... 110
Symptoms of Sleep Problems ............................................ 111
Sleep Deprivation to the Life-Saving PAP Device ............ 111
Diagnosed with Insomnia Disorder ................................... 115

## Chapter 9: Obsessive-Compulsive Disorder (OCD) ............... 117
Excessive Hand Washing ................................................... 118
Overzealous Cleaning ........................................................ 119
Checking Behaviour ........................................................... 119
Counting .............................................................................. 120
Organization ....................................................................... 120
Fears of Violence ................................................................ 121
Unwanted Sexual Thoughts ............................................... 121
Dwelling on Relationships ................................................. 122
Seeking Reassurance ........................................................ 122
OCD and Me ........................................................................ 122
An Obsession with Potholes .............................................. 124

## Chapter 10: Anger .................................................................... 125
What Is Anger? .................................................................... 127
Why Are Some People Angrier Than Others? .................. 127
Soft Answers Remove Anger. Rough Words Raise Rage. .. 128
Anger and Love ................................................................... 129
Trying to Fix it Myself ......................................................... 130

## Chapter 11: Self-Esteem ......................................................... 131
Where Does Self-Esteem Come From? ............................. 131
What if My Self-Esteem is Low? ........................................ 133
What is Self-Esteem? ......................................................... 134
How to Understand Self-Actualization .............................. 135
High School a Complete Wreck ......................................... 136
I was Bullied at School ....................................................... 137

## Chapter 12: Suicidal Feelings ................................................. 139
### Having Suicidal Thoughts ......................................................... 141
### What Are Suicidal Feelings? ..................................................... 148
### Myths and Misconceptions About Suicidal Feelings ...................... 149
### Is Suicide Selfish? .................................................................... 149
### How Can I Help Someone with Suicidal Feelings? ........................ 150
### How Can I Cope Right Now? ..................................................... 151
### Five Steps to Recovery ............................................................ 152
### Suicide is not the Answer ........................................................ 153
### We Are More Powerful Then We Know ....................................... 155
### I was a Soldier Once ................................................................ 157

## REFERENCES ................................................................................ 161
## Why I Wrote This Book ................................................................. 167

# DEDICATION

This book is dedicated to all the veterans and first responders, both past and present, who have given their time to protect our country, and in memory of the ones who gave all, answering the call of both duty and pride in our country.

From the bottom of my heart, God Bless.

Too often, we take for granted how lucky we are. Among other things, I'm lucky to have been born in this country, which gave me opportunities and freedoms that many people don't enjoy. What I often take for granted is that our country has many brave people who have served or are currently serving in our military, and throughout the service industries, as first responders and in our population in general. You don't have to serve to have a mental illness.

You've been told that you are broken—that you're damaged goods and should be labeled as victims. I, for one, don't buy it. Truth be told, you are the men and women with the skills, determination, and values to ensure we have dominance in this chaotic world.

A veteran or first responder is someone who, at one point in his/her life, wrote a blank cheque payable to "Canadian Government" for an amount up to and including their life. That is HONOUR, and there are too many people in this world who no longer understand it.

# INTRODUCTION TO MENTAL HEALTH

Mental health refers to our social, psychological, and emotional wellbeing. It is about how we feel, think, and behave. It helps us manage stress, make choices, and relate well with friends, family members, and fellow employees. Mental health is very significant at every stage of life, from childhood through adulthood. However, most individuals, in the course of life, experience mental-health problems that affect thinking, mood, and behaviour (Worden, 2018). Mental health is made up of a range of experiences and situations. This can be an ongoing experience of mental wellbeing through severe and challenging mental disorders, which may affect an individual's overall emotional and psychological condition. Some situations in life, such as grief and financial and personal happiness, which involves the way we feel about ourselves, can lead to depression and anxiety.

A person is said to be in a state of well-being when he/she can realize his/her capabilities and can cope with normal life stresses, work productively and fruitfully, and make positive contributions to society. Most individuals experience mental-health problems through loss of their loved ones. In case they are already suffering from mental-health issues, the trauma of discovering their loved one has just passed away may make the burden strong (Abuse & Administration, 2016). The feeling a person experiences from losing a loved one can range from depression, feelings of hopelessness, loneliness, and suicidal thoughts. Among many factors that contribute to mental-health problems are biological factors, such as genes or brain chemistry. Life experiences, such as losing a loved one, can lead to mental illness due to trauma. Lastly, it can be inherited, especially in families who have a history of mental-health problems. It can be passed from one generation to the next.

# CHAPTER 1

## HOW TO RECOGNIZE MENTAL HEALTH

It is challenging to distinguish normal mental health from mental disorder, because there is no easy test that shows when something is wrong with our mental health. Primary mental-health conditions can be mimicked by physical ailments (Mond, 2014). Mental-health conditions are not caused by physical disorders, and they can be diagnosed and treated regarding signs and symptoms, as well as how the state impacts an individual's daily activities. A mental-health condition can affect individual behaviour. Most individuals experiencing difficult life situations, which may alter their mental health sometimes, tend to show strange practices, such as obsessive handwashing and drinking too much alcohol, which can be symptoms of a mental-health issue.

Sometimes healthcare professionals can recognize the mental health of a person through the deep or ongoing sadness and anger they are experiencing. Fixed beliefs that are hard to change in the light of conflicting evidence, accompanied by thoughts of suicidal activity, are signs of a mental-health condition. A person with no mental-health problems will never think of committing suicide. *Diagnostic and Satistical Manual of Mental Health Disorders* was published to demonstrate signs and symptoms associated with mental disorders. Healthcare professionals make use of this system to diagnose everything from anorexia to voyeurism, and determine the appropriate treatment. Using an individual's perception, healthcare professionals can recognize the mental-health status of a person, depending on how much an individual's signs and symptoms affect their daily life activities. For instance, you may recognize that you are not doing well, or that you don't want to do the things you used to enjoy doing. This results in a person feeling sad, hopeless, and discouraged.

If your sadness is due to a specific cause, such as loss of employment, your feelings could be healthy and are termed a "temporary reaction." However, if the symptoms persevere, you should seek medical attention, because they can result in depression (Hom, Stanley & Joiner, 2015). To determine if you are mentally healthy, you should not rely on your perceptions alone to articulate your behaviour, thoughts, and ability to function. Other people, such as friends and family members, are essential to understanding if your response is normal and healthy. For example, most people with bipolar disorder seem to confuse it with normal moods swings, which are part of the regular ups and downs of life. However, your thoughts and actions might appear abnormal to people around you.

Individuals who experience severe signs and symptoms of a mental-health condition are advised to seek medical care. For example, when a person is thinking of committing suicide and has extreme mood swings, which result in excessive anger, hostility, and violent behaviour. Individuals who are not able to cope with challenges experienced in daily activities should also seek medical care.

# CHAPTER 1: HOW TO RECOGNIZE MENTAL HEALTH

## How Mental Health Relates to Depression

Current research, which was conducted by the Social Care Institute for Excellence (SCIE), suggests that one person in six who are experiencing mental-health problems will become depressed at some point in their life. It is therefore clear that mental health is linked to depression (Pantic, 2014). Existing mental-health conditions and depression can diminish the quality of life, and can also lead to more extended illnesses, which can worsen an individual's health status.

This condition also generates an economic cost to society, due to lost work productivity and increased healthcare costs. Understanding the relationship between mental health and depression is the first step in developing strategies to reduce the co-existing conditions and support those who are already living with a mental illness. Depression is a mental-health problem that can affect anyone at every stage of life, from every background and occupation.

When healthcare professionals are categorizing individuals who are experiencing depression, they make judgments that determine the cut-off point of the continuum of mental-health illness, which is socially constructed. Even though physical problems sometimes cause depression, mental-health conditions play a significant contributing factor to depression. People who have mental-health problems are at very high risk of losing their jobs, so they lack stable housing and are at risk for experiencing social isolation (Mond, 2014). This is a very challenging situation, which if not taken care of, can leave a person depressed.

People living with mental-health problems experience emotion distress, which leads to the development of depression and anxiety. Mental health and depression share many signs and symptoms, such as physical impairment, hallucinations, anxiety, and intellectual impairment. People with significant psychiatric disorders, such as depression, are at very high risk of developing a range of chronic physical conditions, which affect every biological system in the body, leading to life-threatening illnesses such as obesity and diabetes.

## How Mental Health Affects Family, Friends, and Co-Workers

Mental-health conditions can create harrowing and traumatic times for all family members and have a huge impact on the family's financial and emotional component. When it comes to mental-health illness, the emotional and behavioral consequences to a family member go mostly ignored. An individual's mental health can have a huge impact on others, especially family members (Ibrahim & Ohtsuka, 2014). Looking after a family member who has a mental-health problem is stressful, and as a person tries to cope with this stress, it leads to an increase of physical problems, such as fatigue and loss of appetite.

A study has indicated that half of family members claimed to have developed social and psychological issues while taking care of their relatives with mental-health problems, to the extent that they need help and support. Family life becomes unsettled and unpredictable as the needs of their sick relative becomes paramount. In some cases, some family members are forced to leave their jobs to take care of their loved one, which affects the financial status of the family. Friendship is termed a significant element of protecting our mental health. We should talk to our friends about the challenges we are experiencing, and we should listen to them. When someone has a mental-health problem or is experiencing psychological distress, it is important to keep the friendships ongoing, even though people with mental illness do not like interacting with others.

Healthcare professionals state that friendship is a crucial component that can help someone live with or recover quickly from mental-health problems and overcome the isolation that comes with it (O'Neil et al. 2014). The most common types of mental-health illnesses experienced at the workplace include depression, anxiety, and bipolar disorder. If your co-worker is depressed, he/she may experience unpredictable mood swings (Penning & Wu, 2015). The only way to help these individuals is by encouraging them to talk and treating what they say with respect. Co-workers should encourage people with mental-health problems to seek support from the workplace.

If we could spread our love as quickly as we spread our hate
and negativity,

what a beautiful world we would live in.

# My Swiss Air Flight 111 – Trauma Never Ends

*John A. MacDonald presented his story to an open forum at the University of PEI.*

http://www.cbc.ca/news/canada/prince-edward-island/ptsd-led-to-suicidal-thoughts-says-p-e-i-man-1.2639526

*Good evening, everyone. My name is John MacDonald, and before I get into my story, I would like to tell you a little about my background. I grew up on this great island and joined the army when I was seventeen. For the next twenty-four years, I would travel this world. While living in Truro NS, in 1996, I joined the Central Colchester Ground Search and Rescue Team. I have a few pointers I would like to pass on to any of you out there heading out to an accident scene or come across a traumatic event. These lessons learned came at a cost to me, as I was diagnosed with Severe PTSD two years ago. But I feel it is my time to pass them along to you, even if only one of you remember them.*

*In September of 1998, Swiss Air Flt 111, went down off Peggy's Cove. Our Team was called out. I went on several searches there, but nothing compared to what transpired on Sept 20, 1998. Anyone in here who has PTSD can tell you the exact date, and every small detail about their event, because we live it in our heads daily. On that morning, two eighteen-year-old high school lads on my Truro team, a lady from the Halifax team, and a new-to-us team leader from Halifax, as well as myself, were asked to go into the briefing tent. We were told that, shortly, us five would get on a helicopter and head out to Pearl Island. I never heard of Pearl Island before that day, but I can tell you, it is now etched in my mind. The Mountie told us that this small island was directly behind the crash site, and that no search team had been out there yet. So, a bit of fear was then set in our minds. We then were given body bags, specimen bags, garbage bags, and moved over to Peggy's Cove parking lot to await the chopper.*

*As we lifted off over the iconic lighthouse, the sun was coming up, and it was a beautiful fall day. But all that beauty would end shortly. The flight took only about twenty minutes. The chopper then went low around the island. We were all looking out the doors as the pilot banked to the right. It was then that we see the mess, very clearly. The pilot then said, "You guys are not going to have a good*

## CHAPTER 1: HOW TO RECOGNIZE MENTAL HEALTH

*day, and you're not in Kansas anymore." I looked over at the lady on the team; she looked white, and she then said over her headset that she would not be getting out of the chopper. We then landed in the centre, unloaded, and us four got out. We then headed to the bank, but then the unthinkable happened. Our team leader froze in the centre of the island and said he would not be going to join us. This really threw the three of us left. But we had to carry on.*

*So, these two teens and I were now on our own, chopper gone, team leader and another team member out of the picture. If you are going to an event, hopefully you will have a strong team and team leader, who will support and talk prior, on route and on site, to check in on your feelings, and to see how everyone on the team is coping. Small words mean so much currently, like "How you are doing? Are things good?" and taking breaks. And this check in must be ongoing. As you see, this did not happen with us.*

*As us three approached the bank and stood there, we all froze at the scene before us. There was stuff everywhere. Pieces of the aircraft, burnt wires, clothes, toys, and more. It was at this point that I had to use my military leadership, and I said to the young lads, "We can do this together." So, we headed into it and started picking. I have to say, emotionally, it was one of the hardest days of my life, and we went nonstop for the next ten hours. We stuck close together, as we made our way around. I provided emotional support to the young lads, and they to me.*

*We all had our moments that day. We all broke down, including myself. Around one bend, I seen something that my mind could not register. It was half an aircraft seat, with some other pieces and a stuffed teddy beside it. It was at this point that I sat and broke down. But as I say, the three of us showed each other a lot of support, and the young lads came to my rescue and we all sat and talked for a bit. Our day was only half over by then, and we continued to place black garbage bags up on the bank. But with continually talking and checking on each other, as well as a little black humour, we carried on.*

*We all know that what we would find there this day could be vital to the overall investigation. I was nearing the end of our search when we found it. I will not go into detail. But I will say that we brought a part of a crash victim back with us that day to Peggy's Cove. This was another very tough event for us, but we knew that it was very likely to happen. It was dark, when the helicopter picked us up and we returned to Peggy's Cove. We were emotionally drained. We dropped all our garbage bags, and our other victim, to the RMCP forensics Team. It was good* in a way to know that, along with all the bags full of pieces we found, that some family member, who was on the plane would now be identified. On our return, the team captain was then removed from the search area. A couple of months later I was given a Letter of Commendation from the RCMP for my actions that day, but little did I know that Swiss Air, for the next two years, would consume, eat me up, and nearly ruin my life.

As anyone here with PTSD will tell you, life after a trauma is consumed by their events. For me, life became all things Swiss Air. I did not realize it then, but I had all the PTSD symptoms then. I did not seek out help then. In the two years that followed, I would lose my marriage, children, turn to partying, drinking, and financial ruin. And in the end, one lonely night, it almost took me. Thank God, it was at this point that I met a beautiful lady who saved me, and my life. I call her my angel. But life went on for fourteen more years, with my nightmares, restless nights, living in a confused world, always being paranoid, and loosening my temper very fast at the smallest things. And the monsters were always there. I knew I had to get help, and reached out to the military OSSIS group, and started to see an awesome psychologist. I know my PTSD will never end. Some days are worse than others. I like to explain it as this little monster, a stuck memory that is spinning on one of those little wire wheels in my head. Some days he is quiet, but a lot of the time he is spinning fast. I have a few triggers: helicopters, lighthouses, black garbage bags… I do fly in a plane, but sometimes it's not easy. But seeking help has practically saved my life.

I think my main lessons I learned that day and would like to pass to you is this:

- Have a strong team, even if it is only you and your partner. Continually check in on each other by talking about your feelings, before, during, and after the crisis. Feelings need to be talked about.
- If you feel something has bothered you, or continues to, talk to your work's crisis peer trained personnel. Or if you do not have one setup at your job, seek out help, or PSTD groups. Do not let it eat you up, because it will.

CHAPTER 1: HOW TO RECOGNIZE MENTAL HEALTH

## The Days We Should Not Worry

———

There are two days in every week about which we should not worry—two days which should be kept free from fear and apprehension.

One of those days is yesterday, with all its mistakes and cares,

its faults and blunders, its aches and pain.

Yesterday has passed forever beyond our control. All the money in the world cannot bring back yesterday.

We cannot undo a single act we performed. We cannot erase a single word we said. Yesterday is gone forever.

The other day we should not worry about is tomorrow, with all its possible adversities, its burden, its lazy promise, and its poor performance. Tomorrow is also beyond our immediate control.

Tomorrow's sun will rise, either in splendour or behind a mask of clouds, but it will rise. Until it does, we have no stake in tomorrow, for it is yet to be born.

This only leaves one day: today. Every person fights the battle of just one day. It is when you and I add the burden of those two awful eternities, yesterday and tomorrow, that we breakdown.

# CHAPTER 2

## POST-TRAUMATIC STRESS DISORDER

Post-traumatic stress disorder (PTSD) is a psychological disorder associated with adverse consequences. This chapter discusses the post-traumatic stress disorder concerned with the military and first responders in conflict and war. This is because the condition is common among personnel, indicating that it is necessary that the causes, symptoms, and discussion strategies are outlined accordingly. The most common symptoms of PTSD include arousal, hopelessness about the future, a lack of positive thinking, and thinking of the traumatic event most of the time. There are various practices that can be employed to prevent PTSD, including using positive emotions and laughter to avoid attack from thoughts and stress, helping others in their healing process to prevent thoughts of people suffering, sharing thoughts and feelings to their loved ones, and considering recovery from the tragedy as a survivor and not a victim for change in thoughts. Such practices are essential in minimizing and preventing PTSD amongst military personnel. We don't see our lives as they are; we see our lives worse than they are.

Post-traumatic stress disorder is a mental illness or an impact of trauma that disturbs the behaviour, feelings, and thoughts of a person—the way a person thinks and the way a person functions typically. Post-traumatic stress disorder is commonly caused by traumatic events. Trauma is a deeply distressing or disturbing experience from war, conflict, and other terrifying events. PTSD can be realized using symptoms of change in physical and mental reactions named in this article. Unlike other mental disorders, PTSD usually has an onset point and what triggers it, and the symptoms of PTSD typically develop days after the tragedy; which help the EMTs to detect survivors who could be diagnosed with PTSD, and provide prevention techniques for future use. Even though these techniques have been introduced, there are no clear ways of preventing PTSD, because there are several barriers to seeking the help of the research for affected individuals. It explains the meaning of post-traumatic stress disorder and touches on the PTSD of first responders such as police, firefighters, emergency medical teams, and other responders to the war and conflict, or the daily business on home soil. The examination of the causes and effects of trauma in the above categories of people is conducted. Some of the discussed reasons include war and conflict, deaths, and terrorist attacks. The symptoms and ways of how to deal with PTSD are also outlined.

## PTSD for Military and First Responders

PTSD generally occurs after a traumatic experience or after severe chronic situations. People who witness natural disasters, such as floods, fire calamities, and those losing their loved ones from accidents, terrorist attacks, and personal assaults such as rape, are mostly affected by PTSD. The prevalence of traumatic stress is significantly high. The approximated number varies, depending on factors like stress, age, gender, mental or physical health condition, the type of trauma, marital status, and serious accidents as well as house fires (Hoge et al., 2014). People usually react differently to fatal or unexpected incidents. Some people might respond to events as a shock or become overwhelmed, while others respond to the same event amazed and feeling grateful.

# CHAPTER 2: POST-TRAUMATIC STRESS DISORDER

In the military, PTSD has been reported to affect women twice as much as men. The reason is that women are generally known to be more prone to trauma compared to their counterparts. Women can be abused, depressed due to rejection and the general injustices they go through, and because they break down so quickly, they end up being affected by PTSD (Vujanovic et al., 2013). There are some forms of PTSD that have distinct features and are specific within the diagnosis of PTSD. Some of the factors include dissociative and delayed onset or expression, where someone experiences the onset of some symptoms of trauma more immediately, but the full symptoms are experienced after six months. In the dissociative type, someone observes that something is not real, where someone feels unfamiliar or disconnected from the world around him or her. post–traumatic stress disorder is common among military personnel such as firefighters, police, and the emergency medical teams (EMTs) (Trimble, 2013).

Post-traumatic stress disorder has been noted severally among the Canadian and US soldiers reporting high levels of psychological stress. Even the highly respected soldiers from the Canadian military, Lieutenant General Romeo Dallaire and Lieutenant Colonel Stephan Grenier, have been associated with PTSD in their career endeavours. However, PTSD is not limited to soldiers. PTSD can also develop in other first responders exposed to traumatic experiences. The first responders here refer to the EMTs, police, firefighters, and the people concerned with the lives of their loved ones (Figley, 2013). Combatants as first responders experience a lot during their operation to stop or aid a war conflict. They see friends/colleague laying there with their internal organs exposed, others killed, or others catching fire. Other soldiers experience the traumatic events themselves, in person, threatened with death, confrontations with insurgents, catching fire, or scars resulting from the war. When some of their close friends go through hard times during the war conflict, a soldier can also be affected by trauma later.

A soldier may have PTSD when the experience he/she has gone through continues for more than a month and causes changes in the ability to think normally and impacts negatively their social life. These negative changes may include negative beliefs about themselves or others, blaming themselves for a particular result, persistence in feelings, alterations of attitudes towards people that are usually close, and losing interest in things that one usually loves doing. According to Steenkamp and Litz, (2013), one also experiences a lack of sleep due to a lot of thoughts and a drop of concentration toward the people around them. They become anxious and sensitive to their surroundings and keep scanning the environment for possible threats. Being sensitive to their surroundings causes them to have different behaviour and to give attention to things other than their families.

Police officers also undergo several events that can cause PTSD. They often go to traumatic scenes where shootings or deaths have occurred. When police officers go through these, they can become affected, and this impairs their mentality and ability to work generally for the public. They can't deliver their usual duties to the people well, because of the previous traumatic events. According to Figley (2013), police officers, due to the mental impacts from the earlier scenes, cannot be right in decision making for the safety of the public. One may also change in their behaviour such that he/she may begin abusing substances or may have thoughts of committing suicide. Police officers experiencing PTSD have been reported not to be competent while executing their professional duties, due to repercussions of psychological disorders.

## CHAPTER 2: POST-TRAUMATIC STRESS DISORDER

Firefighters and the emergency medical teams (EMTs) experience the same post-trauma because they engage in the act of saving people affected by armed conflicts and war. Some of the victims pass while being treated at triage. Firefighters see a lot of people burn inside a building, and yet the best they can do is stop the fire. Some of the victims are rescued when already burnt. Some of the firefighters have been burned while rescuing the victims. These responders end up with PTSD, because they see a lot of people suffering from the impacts of war. They witness the deaths of people, and they end up having long-term exposure to trauma and high levels of stress (Hoge et al., 2014).

## Symptoms of Post-Traumatic Stress Disorder and Treatment

The symptoms of PTSD can be categorized as arousal, hopelessness about the future, lack of positive thinking, and thinking of the traumatic event most of the time. The arousal signs are always being cautious of the environment, a lack of sleep due to a loss of concentration, feeling ashamed, and having aggressive behaviour (Figley, 2013). There are various situations that lead to hopelessness and negative thoughts about the future such as losing a friend during a battle or losing a friend who is in your rescue team. The military personnel usually get afraid when such occurrences happen to their colleagues, a factor which can cause PTSD.

PSTD is also characterized by a lack of positive thinking, the inability to make the best of things. Thinking of how the events unfolded and how they ended is another symptom that leads to PTSD. One should get close to their loved ones to avoid thoughts of the terrifying events. According to Bisson et al., (2013), these symptoms vary in intensity and from person to person. In this case, intensity symptoms may be higher when one has encountered a traumatic experience and become stressed generally. For example, one may watch news of a traumatic scene similar to what he/she went through, and become occupied with thinking of his/her own experience. This symptom is treated by avoiding watching these traumatic scenes.

One may also have suicidal thoughts after a traumatic experience. This should be treated by talking to a friend or loved ones, contacting a spiritual leader, visiting a mental-health doctor, or even counselling offices near you and getting emergency help by calling availed helplines (Figley, 2013). Such techniques are essential in helping military personnel avoid psychological disorders in their career endeavours.

## Prevention of Post-Traumatic Stress Disorder

It is hard for human beings to prevent pain and suffering. One can only avoid the negative impacts of the illnesses. Post-traumatic stress disorder can be prevented by using positive emotions and laughter to avert an attack from thoughts and stress, helping others in their healing process to avoid thoughts of people suffering, sharing thoughts and feelings with loved ones, and considering his recovery from the tragedy as a survivor and not a victim for a change in thoughts (Vujanovic et al., 2013). It is also recommended that one holds beliefs that help in managing feelings and accepting the pain and suffering from traumatic events as lessons for the future.

PTSD is a common psychological problem that is prevalent in all corners of the world. The disorder is associated with several adverse effects that make the victims lead miserable lives. Previously conducted studies have reported PTSD to be most prevalent amongst the military, firefighters, police, and the emergency medical teams (EMTs), both serving and retired. The most common symptoms of PTSD include arousal, hopelessness about the future, lack of positive thinking, and thinking of the traumatic event most of the time. There are various practices that can be employed to prevent PTSD, including using positive emotions and laughter to avoid attack from thoughts and stress, helping others in their healing process to prevent thoughts of people suffering, sharing thoughts and feelings with loved ones and considering their recovery from the tragedy as a survivor and not a victim, changing their thoughts. Such practices are essential in helping military personnel lead happy lives.

There are several significant ways that the management of first responders and militaries can work on PTSD. The best way to work on this, of course, is

## CHAPTER 2: POST-TRAUMATIC STRESS DISORDER

preventing it before it develops in the officers. There should be training done on trauma awareness, training in ways of increasing mental flexibility, and mental-health training for first responders and military officers.

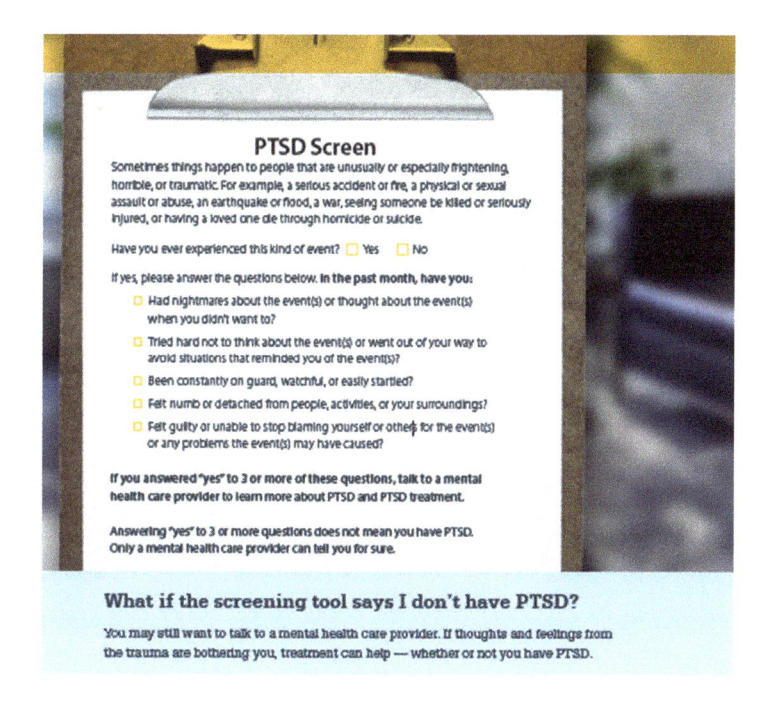

### PTSD Screen

Sometimes things happen to people that are unusually or especially frightening, horrible, or traumatic. For example, a serious accident or fire, a physical or sexual assault or abuse, an earthquake or flood, a war, seeing someone be killed or seriously injured, or having a loved one die through homicide or suicide.

Have you ever experienced this kind of event? ☐ Yes ☐ No

If yes, please answer the questions below. In the past month, have you:

- ☐ Had nightmares about the event(s) or thought about the event(s) when you didn't want to?
- ☐ Tried hard not to think about the event(s) or went out of your way to avoid situations that reminded you of the event(s)?
- ☐ Been constantly on guard, watchful, or easily startled?
- ☐ Felt numb or detached from people, activities, or your surroundings?
- ☐ Felt guilty or unable to stop blaming yourself or others for the event(s) or any problems the event(s) may have caused?

If you answered "yes" to 3 or more of these questions, talk to a mental health care provider to learn more about PTSD and PTSD treatment.

Answering "yes" to 3 or more questions does not mean you have PTSD. Only a mental health care provider can tell you for sure.

**What if the screening tool says I don't have PTSD?**

You may still want to talk to a mental health care provider. If thoughts and feelings from the trauma are bothering you, treatment can help — whether or not you have PTSD.

### *USA National Center for PTSD*
www.ptsd.va.gov

19

## A Share by a Lineman Brother of Mine, A Senior NCM in the Lineman trade. Lead by Example

*After thirty plus years of service, you have a lot of great memories and many friends that we are glad to call brothers. You also have many times of not-so-great memories. My tour in Bosnia was as a senior NCO (Warrants Officer), and although the fighting was in peace negotiations, the threat of violence was from a local who was drunk on slevo and didn't believe in peace, and the ever-present land mines. I would not have any of my troops put into any situation that I wouldn't go into myself. There were many occasions where I had to send troops to do projects that could put them in harm's way. I did go with them as a leader, but they were very inexperienced in the way of dealing with foreign troops that could be belligerent. Most of them were on their first deployment, so I had to teach them and take care of them.*

*My next deployment (2008-09) was into Kandahar Airfield in Kandahar Province (KAF) as everyone called it. I was part of Regional Command South (RC South), and although part of the Canadian contingent, I had a troop of Dutch soldiers who would carry out the work, as RC South was under Dutch command. Once again, I took them under my wing, as this was an active fighting area with threats all around. Our first project outside the wire, we went with the Dutch Force Protection convoy. Anytime outside the wire is dangerous, everything from IEDs to SVBIED (suicide vehicle born improvised explosive device) trying to infiltrate the convoy. Our convoy was no exception. The good thing is we got them before they got us. Our Dutch lead armored vehicle engaged the usual "white Toyota" as it made a high-speed approach, with a .50 Cal. round into the engine block to disable it. How do you protect your troops from something like that? There were many more occasions outside the wire where I made it a point to be with the troops in case something was to happen. Whether or not I could do anything was not the point. I had to be there. If I had to send them out, I couldn't live with the fact that they were injured or killed, and I could have done something. Our last time outside the wire was set up for my replacement to see one of the FOBs (Forward Operation Base). I had it arranged for a helicopter to get them there for additional security, as you are not on the road. When it came time*

## CHAPTER 2: POST-TRAUMATIC STRESS DISORDER

*for the project, my replacement was too sick to go out, so the job still had to get done, so guess who's going out one more time?*

*When I get to the hanger to get the helicopter, I am told it's been reassigned to a higher priority location and we were now traveling by a US convoy to our location. If you don't know or haven't figured it out, the Americans are very quick to engage with the enemy, and they pose a big target on the road. I remember getting into the back of the AMRAP (armored mine resistant armored personal carrier), telling my troops everything will be fine, and then hearing the voice of Peter Mansbridge announcing on the National about another Canadian soldier dying as the result of an IED two days before going home. This is the last thing I remember from that convoy, and to this day, I cannot listen to Peter Mansbridge.*

*Now I am deployed to Kabul, the capital of Afghanistan, in 2013 for the closing of the Canadian mission in Afghanistan. This time I oversee Canadian troops, and I **will not** let anything happen to them! If you have any knowledge about Kabul, you know it is a city designed for less than a million people but has around two plus million living and driving anything and everything from cars to mules with carts. Everything you have been taught about "staying safe" in country cannot be done, as the minute you leave the relative safety of the base, you are facing an onslaught of traffic and street vendors with their pressure cookers and propane tanks along roadside streets, high dirt walls with holes in them allowing for easy sniper access. Disturbed earth everywhere along the roadside, and traffic that is almost always at a complete standstill most of the time. Again against everything we are taught and told to avoid at all cost.*

*So, as we sit in the traffic with who knows who beside you, behind you, ahead of your convoy, just waiting for you, you're going over almost every possible scenario in your head trying to calculate how to push through the shit storm that may befall us at any second. As this was a closure mission, we had to be outside the wire many times to close FOBs from all the Canadian content, and each time we rolled the dice and wondered if this was the time we would not come back.*

*Several other "hazards" on the road were the children who threw rocks, but with an AK47 on their back, and the old wailing lady with the "baby" in the middle of the road, forcing traffic off the roads into God knows what. How can one expect to do that again and again under constant stress, all the while trying to ensure no one gets hurt or killed, then just come back home to real life again?*

*It has taken me a long time to write even this much. I struggle every day with driving, crowds, hyper vigilance, loud noises, and anger issues. Nightmares, no sleep, or waking at three a.m. are also constant in my life.*

*As the title suggests, this is my struggle as a leader to not only do the job but do it and bring home the troops, so no one must get that knock on the door by the unit padres, that your son, daughter, husband, wife etc. will not be coming back to you. How do you do that and expect them to do all the heavy lifting while you sit in your glass tower and direct them like players in a game? That's not how it works for me. I brought all my troops home but live with the aftermath on my mental health every day.*

*Phil.*

## Story Share by Author
## Camp Butmir – The Demons

*It was coming to the end of the tour and the logistical part of it was to repatriate all the soldiers back home to their hometowns. We were called in groups to the main theatre, located in the NATO (North Atlantic Treaty Organization) HQ building. The briefing started and a medical nurse was standing off to the side. When it was her turn to speak, she walked up to the podium and ask all present, "Does anyone suffer from PTSD?"*

*We all started to look around at each other, knowing we had something running around inside our heads (little demons); however, being hardened soldiers, we all said, "No!" laughing it off. Knowing that, if we did, we would be treated, and a label attached. We were told by the senior officers that, if we stated that we had PTSD, your career would be over in the army, no postings and no promotions. They went on to say, "Good luck getting a job. You won't even be allowed to drive a school bus, so suck it up, soldier." The papers ...not sure what we signed, but apparently, we signed papers stating we did not have PTSD. This happened in the summer of 2001, not knowing what PTSD was, even though we all came back with demons in our heads.*

*I was drawn back to Camp Butmir, Sarajevo, Bosnia & Herzegovina in 2003 and 2005. They were for different missions. In 2003, I was working for NATO,*

## CHAPTER 2: POST-TRAUMATIC STRESS DISORDER

*Operation Palladium, and 2005 was for European Force, Operation Athena. Nonetheless, the risk and hostility were still high, and the mental stress was sometimes overwhelming.*

*I was assigned to support the task force as the line team chief, and one of the duties was to lead a multinational team consisting of US Marines, Army, and Air Force, Dutch Army, Italian Army, Turkish Army, and of course, our Canadian Lineman. This was stressful, as we supported all of the Bosnia & Herzegovina and Croatia, constantly sending out teams from the camp, knowing the risk and the hostility was present, and hoping all returned, was a whole different stress all by itself.*

*I decided to go along on my trips, and leaving the 2 I/C in command, in a way, I felt personally responsible to ensure their safe return.*

*It's a different lifestyle. Waking up in the morning and strapping your pistol to your leg and throwing a couple of clips on your belt, all before breakfast, was the normal routine. We were busy almost every day, right up to bedtime, which helps pass the day quickly; however, some days never ended, when you lose a colleague due to an IED (improvised explosive device—a bomb constructed and deployed in ways other than conventional military action) or sad, disappointing letters from home of spouses or partners leaving them.*

*One day, a soldier who received a letter stating that his girlfriend had run off with his best friend and sold all his stuff, was devastated. He did not show any signs to make his direct sergeant worry. The "barracks" living quarters were constructed to have a life span of ten to fifteen years maximum, so the walls and infrastructure were extremely thin. It was two stories tall with wings going left and right, with ten rooms per wing and a centralized community bathroom. That night, the soldier went back to his room, sat on his bed, took out his pistol, put it to his head, and pulled the trigger. The bullet went through his head then proceeded to enter the next room upstairs, and finally ending up in a soldier's back upstairs. The bullet lodged itself in the soldier upstairs, and he bled out. As all soldiers are on a call 24/7, it was part of the operational plan that all soldiers kept rifles, pistols, and ammunition in their rooms.*

*Camp Butmir had 1200 soldiers from 32 Nations, most of us seeing things we don't even tell of—something no man or woman should ever see. Canadians had soldiers with PTSD, anxiety, anger, sleep disorders, and addictions. These*

23

*soldiers only spoke of these demons behind closed doors and to a small community of friends, as the senior leadership frowned on mental-health issues.*

*Prior to the conflict in Bosnia & Herzegovina, Canada sold millions on POM3 (anti-personnel mines) to the former Yugoslavia. These anti-personnel mines were the size of a large hockey puck, and the design intent was to remove the leg up to the knee. This was a strategy. If a soldier went down due to a mine, it would take two soldiers to carry him. There was more POM3 installed in Bosnia & Herzegovina than in Cambodia.*

*In Camp Butmir, our team stored our material and telecommunication equipment in a HAS (hardened air shelter). This was a bunker to hide small aircraft. It was a half circle above ground, one-foot-thick concrete, twenty feet high in the center, and covered in clay and grass approximately two feet thick. One day,*

*our internet was down and since we had an office in the HAS for our materials NCM, a corporal and me were up on the HAS, fixing the connection to enable our internet again. A couple days later, we encountered a huge rainstorm and two POM3 washed down the side of the hill, from the same vicinity where we had been working. The biggest, sickest feeling I ever had engulphed my stomach. Keep in mind, this area was swept for mines prior to NATO occupying it; however, checks are 90 percent at best.*

## Story Share by Anonymous
## Suffering from Nightmares and Panic Attacks

*When I was younger, I heard of PTSD for the first time in a history classroom where the teacher described it as "shell shock." I remember seeing a picture of a gaunt figure lying in bed. I wondered at the time what he had been through in the trenches that made him feel like that. I never thought I would have experienced something like that in my wildest dreams.*

*I am twenty-two. I drink tea, sing, knit, and am training to be a secondary-school teacher. I also suffer from PTSD, depression, and anxiety. I am recovering, but recovery is never meant to be easy.*

*When I was sixteen, I got on a train. I remember the newspapers around me explaining the elation we as Londoners felt in the Olympics. I remember feeling happy, but that train was to change my life. I was on one of the trains that was attacked in 7.7. I survived but had no scratches. I went home covered in soot and tried to forget about it.*

*I started to suffer from nightmares and panic attacks. I used to hate being around smoke and people who were covered in fake blood. Even now, I refuse to use a certain exit at King's Cross station, because it reminds me of that day. It broke me down very quickly. I found surviving was the hardest thing I ever had to do. Every day was a struggle, and sometimes still is, forcing myself to get out of bed when I have spent all night with nightmares is agonizing. I remember thinking, and I used to be ashamed of this, that living was the hardest thing. Sometimes, I thought that it would have been easier if I was killed that day.*

*This has left me with severe trust issues; I do not let anyone in, even a doctor. I have tried and failed, often too scared to attend appointments. I find it hard to* love, and to trust despite the fact I am trying to be so caring. I try and prevent other people feeling upset, because I don't want them to feel anything near or like what I did. I often suffer in silence, and sometimes people have asked me if I am okay. My response is 'I'm fine' when in fact I want to scream out that everything is not okay. Frankly, I don't want them to worry. But I am also afraid that I will be told to 'Grow up' or 'Get over' this. I can't do that easily, sadly. I don't think anyone can ever understand these illnesses unless they go through it, but I will do my best to explain to them how hard it is. That's if I trust them enough to hear how I feel in the first place.

But this illness is not me, and nor does it make me. It is a part of me. Yes, I suffer from these dreams and these feelings, but I have friends, and slowly, I am beginning to rebuild my life. I have allowed myself to love people again and let myself enter a profession where I must be strong. I don't think I could have done that six years ago. I am not strong, but nor am I weak. I have been through things that people cannot imagine, but then for me this is normal. For me, it's something I must learn to live with, and hopefully with time and some courage (to ask for help), I will be okay.

I cannot remember who I was before that train; it's such a turning point in my life, but I have made it out the other side. That is why I am writing this blog: to tell people that things will get better. I hope I can inspire at least one person to go and ask for help, because mental illness does not make you, nor is it you. But it's just one aspect in someone's wonderful personality.

## Story Share by Anonymous
## Trying to Raise a Family with PTSD

*He was a thirty-six-year-old married veteran who had returned from Afghanistan, where he had served as an officer. He went to the Veterans Affairs outpatient mental-health clinic complaining of having "a short fuse" and being "easily triggered."*

*His symptoms involved out-of-control rage when startled, constant thoughts and memories of death-related events, weekly vivid nightmares of combat that caused trouble sleeping, anxiety, and a loss of interest in hobbies he once enjoyed with friends.*

## CHAPTER 2: POST-TRAUMATIC STRESS DISORDER

*Although all these symptoms were very distressing, he was most worried about his extreme anger. His "hair-trigger temper" caused fights with drivers who cut him off, cursing at strangers who stood too close in checkout lines, and shifts into "attack mode" when coworkers startled him by accident. In a recent visit to the doctor, he was drifting off to sleep on the exam table. A nurse brushed by his foot, and he leapt up, cursing and threatening her—scaring both the nurse and him.*

*He kept a handgun in his car for self-protection, but he had no intent to harm others. He had deep remorse after a threatening incident and worried that he might accidentally hurt someone.*

*These moments reminded him of a time in the military when he was on guard at the front gate. While he was dozing, an enemy mortar round stunned him into action.*

*He was raised in a loving family that struggled to make ends meet as Midwestern farmers. At age twenty, he joined the U.S. Army and deployed to Afghanistan. He described himself as having been upbeat and happy before his army service. He said he enjoyed basic training and his first few weeks in Afghanistan, until one of his comrades got killed. At that point, all he cared about was getting his best friend and himself home alive, even if it meant killing others. His personality changed, he said, from that of a happy-go-lucky farm boy to a frightened, overprotective soldier.*

*When he returned to civilian life, he got a college degree and a graduate business degree. He chose to work as a self-employed plumber, because of his need to stay alone in his work. He had been married for seven years and was the father of two young daughters. In his retirement, he looked forward to woodworking, reading, and getting some "peace and quiet."*

*He was diagnosed with post-traumatic stress disorder. His main concerns were his fear and his aggression when startled by someone. He was jittery and always on the lookout for danger. He also had intrusive memories, nightmares, and flashbacks.*

*His attempts to reduce the risk of conflict have reduced his social and career opportunities. For instance, his decision to work as a plumber rather than to use his M.B.A. seemed based largely on his effort to control his personal space.*

## Story Share by Barry
## Leaving the Battlefield.

*I am a soldier and I have PTSD. I refused to admit it to myself even when the army doctors told me I had it in 2004. I refused to talk to anyone about it, even when army health professionals told me I needed to in 2005. I was afraid how army leadership would react if I had that on my record. I was a soldier. I was tough. I just needed to rub the patch and drive on.*

*And drive on I did until one day in September 2010, five years after I last left the battlefield. I don't know what the trigger was. Maybe it was the young soldier, a mother of two, who was just redeployed, who I watched cut down after she hanged herself weeks after returning from battle earlier. Maybe it was the faces of the children I see on all the doors I knocked on to tell them their father or mother was not coming home. Maybe it was because it was the same time of year when my uniform was covered with the blood and brains of a six-year-old Iraqi child who was caught in an IED during Ramadan.*

*I don't know what the trigger was, but it hit me hard. I went home one evening, and all of a sudden, I felt a tightness in my chest. It was hard to breathe. I felt closed in and panicky. I bolted out of bed thinking I was dying. I paced the room in the dark for hours before I exhausted myself. I almost went to the ER that night, but the soldier in me said to stick it out.*

*The morning came and it hit again, a panic, a fear of being closed off, claustrophobia, and pains in my chest. I thought maybe I was having a heart attack, and if I was, I needed to see a doctor.*

*A heart attack was honourable. PTSD was not. I went to sick call and they ordered a battery of tests to exclude any heart condition. When my heart was cleared, the doctors recommended I see someone in CHMS. I thought to myself that I wasn't crazy. "Why do I need to see them? If I see them, I know the 'big' army will find out and tag me as 'broken'."*

*I went home that night and the same thing happened. I knew I could not live like this, so I talked, off the record, to someone in mental health. They looked at my records, and after talking with me, said that I had PTSD. They said there was probably some trigger that set it off. I did not want to believe it, but I knew that I needed something, or I would face the same thing again that evening. I then*

## CHAPTER 2: POST-TRAUMATIC STRESS DISORDER

"*officially*" *saw them and was prescribed some psychotropic medication to help with the anxiety in order to help me function.*

*I thought when I got off the battlefield that I could heal and place the war behind me. As a chaplain, I soon realized that I could not. Within weeks of getting back in 2004, I was knocking on doors telling families that a husband, wife, father, mother, daughter, or son was not coming home. In 2008, I knocked on a door to tell a family that their husband, a father of three, was lost to them. To this day, I can close my eyes and see the face of a teenage daughter who looked at me with hatred. She looked deep into my soul and said that she would never forget what I did to her and her family that day and then turned away, too destroyed to even cry.*

*Even though I was home, I never left the battlefield. I brought the war home, and it took a toll on me and my family, wife, and children. I got to be good friends with Jim and Jack. You may know them as Mr. Beam and Mr. Daniels.*

*I did not want to get close to my new babies for fear I might get deployed again. A big piece of me wanted to go back to battle, because the battlefield made sense; coming home to emails, memorandums, and unit "politics" did not. I also knew that, if I went back, a bigger piece of me did not want to come back home again.*

*The home I came back to was not the one I left. My family was not the same. I was not the same. I felt that something important was stolen from me and there was nobody I could talk to about it. Nobody except the guys I was over there with. I would look for combat patches, look for buddies to talk to, look for the soldiers who went through what I went through and felt the same way I did. There were many of us. Our experiences were very different, but we had one thing in common. We felt different, but we were not crazy or have some defective genetic failing.*

*It just was hard for us to come to terms with all the death, destruction, and pain we had participated in and witnessed. We were all reluctant about "officially" talking to someone. Even if we needed help, we would not go to it, as we thought leadership would use that against us for assignments and promotions.*

*We felt we were alone. We were trapped in our own memories, sometimes trying to ignore them and often not being able to. We watched as our suicide numbers went up and are still going up.*

*The army leadership has tried and is trying to change this trend and is having some success. I cannot say that a piece of me, at one time, did not wonder if the world, my family, would have been off better without me.*

*For soldiers with PTSD, we often felt the very act of seeking help from a mental-health professional could be information that could be used against us, to target us, and make us feel we were burdens to the system. I felt that way and was afraid to get the help I needed. I now fear that the problem may be made worse with the so-called discovery of a PTSD gene. If this data is used wrong or misinterpreted, those of us with PTSD now could be considered genetically dysfunctional.*

*Instead of being a burden to the army, I ended up being a burden to the most important people in my life, my wife and children. Fearing being minimized as a soldier, I, like so many others, went underground. It seemed the very thing that leadership was using to try to help me worked against me.*

*When I close my eyes at night, sometimes I still see myself picking up the body parts of my soldiers. I still see myself holding my soldiers as they die in my arms on the battlefield. I still see the blood of Iraqi children spattered all over my uniform as they take their last breaths due to no fault of their own. In the quiet moments of the day, when I am with my family, I see the faces of all the wives, children, husbands, mothers, and fathers whose lives I destroyed with the notifications I made.*

*My mind tells me that I did not cause their pain and grief, but my heart tells me otherwise. I know I can't change their pain, but I can change mine and the pain I inflicted on my family due to war. Only a soldier understands that physically being home doesn't mean coming home.*

*Coming home from battle seemed to be one of the easiest things to do. It seemed that you just get on a plane. After spending hours, weeks, and months getting help and talking to someone about my wounds, I am only beginning to understand how to come home.*

*I am, in our army culture, what some would identify as a broken or deadwood soldier. I have no bullet holes to show my wounds. I will not get any medal that will recognize them. If I did, I would be afraid and ashamed to wear it in our present culture. As with so many of us, my wounds are the invisible kind, the type we bear in our souls. I am not ashamed of them. For me and others like me, they are just as real as one that bleeds.*

*I am getting help, because I'm tired of not being home. I am tired of being on the battlefield I brought back with me. It is time for me to come home. It is time for all of us to come home. I am not ashamed of my wounds, and I have no genetic failing. I am proud of my service, and I am going home. Let's go home together.*

## CHAPTER 2: POST-TRAUMATIC STRESS DISORDER

# Story Share by Shawn
# My Journey to PTSD and Back

*I wrote this to show those that may be in the same boat as me that there is a way back. This may take a couple of minutes, but please read to the end.*

*It has been two years, and I have come a long way. I am telling a little bit about my personal life so that, as I have been helped, I may be able to help someone. I went to a funeral of a friend of mine in October 2016. We served in the military together and stayed friends since that time. During the funeral, I guess I became overwhelmed and vented to another military friend of mine, Chuck. Chuck just stood there and listened. When I was done, he asked, "Why do you think you can talk to me like that?" Confused at the question, I responded with "You're my friend?" "Yes, I am. And you have PTSD." He then rhymed off all my symptoms. If it were anyone else telling me that, I would have laughed it off, but it was Chuck. Chuck is a veteran and has served in Afghanistan twice. As a commander, he lost some soldiers in the battle against terrorism but also lost some after they came home. He has PTSD and does a great job managing it. If fact, he travels all over Canada helping other soldiers and first responders to understand and manage their injury. He offered to help me, but I was still confused and unsure.*

*I spent the weekend wondering about me having 'it'. I was a tough cop. I came from a military family, served in the military, did a tour of duty in Damascus, joined the corrections service, then became a police officer. I saw a lot, but I was great at dealing with my stress and everything else that came with it. Or so I thought. I talked to my wife and broke down. The tough cop just started crying... I couldn't explain why I broke down, but I did. I would break down many more times after this moment.*

*I know that the many years leading up to this point, I was having numerous flashbacks of the various events I responded to and was having difficulty sleeping. I would review each event in my head as if it was yesterday ... in clear vivid detail. I spent many nights watching TV, trying to stop the show in my head. Many days I would become very frustrated and angry. Driving in traffic, I was the perfect show of someone yelling at nothing in his car. I would 'snap' occasionally, making my home life a difficult one for my family. I know my family would walk on eggshells so as not to get me angry. Although I never became physical, I had that* 'look' which my son called the 'evil eye'. When I became frustrated, I would just throw something or break it, just because. My emotions were all over the place and at times made no sense. My communications skills sucked and were getting worse. At work, I found I was isolating myself more often. I would close the door and stay by myself. I was becoming more suspicious about everything and nothing. I would focus on my work and spend many extra hours doing things so my brain couldn't think about anything else. When I couldn't sleep, I would come to work early just to get my brain busy on something other than the events in my head. Then there was the chronic pain from all the injuries I received over the years. I broke more bones in my last three years patrolling the Downtown East Side than the previous forty years of my life. I was able to hide it all from everyone. I would put on an act… I was "doing great." Look at all the work I accomplished. No one knew I was suffering, not even me. I thought I was just becoming that grumpy old man, and this is the way my life has become. But 'it' was continuing to get worse … not better. Things were piling on.

On my first day back at work, after the funeral, I went to HR, into the Employee Services office where a friend worked, closed the door, and asked for help. I even broke down again. Ann listened and even heard me. She gave me the name of a great psychologist. I set up an appointment the next week and went to see her. I was very nervous, almost scared of possibly being diagnosed with a mental illness. My anxiety level was off the scale. How would that affect me, my career, and how would people react? The stigma is still a large problem in the law-enforcement world. I didn't know what I should do or say when I spoke to her. How should I act? She, Nicole, invited me into her office, and we began my first session. It lasted a few hours. I cried so often I must have looked quite the sight. She had Kleenex right next to my chair, like it was planned, and I used a lot of it. I didn't hold anything back. I told details I never told my wife. I explained what was happening to me and how I acted. And I cried some more. She asked many questions, and I responded with no holds barred. At the end, she gave me a diagnosis. I must have heard wrong, because I remember responding with "So I don't have PTSD?" like I was relieved.

"No. You DO have PTSD."

I remember sitting there thinking about what she was saying and how my life had changed in the last five to seven years or so. Then, it was clear, "Oh thank God. I thought I was going crazy." But I wasn't going crazy. I was changing

## CHAPTER 2: POST-TRAUMATIC STRESS DISORDER

*because of a mental illness that I received through the work I did for the last thirty plus years. I was relieved. I realized that Chuck was right, and I could get help and pulled back from going further down that long dark tunnel. Nicole said she could help me, and we began meeting on a regular basis.*

*I returned to work, went into Ann's office, and informed her of the outcome. It was going to be all good now. Ann began the paperwork for Work Safe BC, and over the next few weeks, began figuring out how she and HR could support and help me. My trip home usually takes forty-five minutes or so, which gave me the time to think about how I would explain this to my family. I had to break it 'easy' because I was telling them that I was vulnerable ... not the tough guy I thought I was. I got home, saw my wife in the kitchen, and broke down again. I explained what had happened, and she hugged me, comforted me, and said we could work on this together. She was there for me. I cried. My son, who was twenty-one at the time, came home. I informed him, and he sat on the edge of the couch looking at me for a few seconds. Then he asked, "So, Dad, how are you?" and hugged me.*

*Over the next two years, I met with Nicole quite a lot. It started as one-on-one, but then she expanded that to include a fellow officer, Mike, who has navigated the dark tunnel with success over the last ten years. We expanded again to group sessions, which I found to be the best for me, as I realized that I was not alone and learned so much from them. When I wasn't meeting with Nicole, Mike and I would meet, and I would vent about my most recent outbursts or breakdowns. He would help me get back up. He was my 'sponsor', my go-to guy, the person I could rely on as he has been there.*

*Both Nicole and Mike helped me so much I don't know how to begin to thank them. I figured knowledge is power or control, so I attended many conferences and seminars on PTSD and Occupational Stress Injuries. My wife and son came with me to some, so they could also learn not only to help me but also to help themselves. I have learned a lot about mental illness and strategies on how to manage it. I will always have PTSD, but now I understand it and can manage quite well. It was not easy though. In the first six months, it felt like things continued to get worse. They weren't worse. I was now recognizing my triggers and all my symptoms daily. Both Nicole and Mike explained that was normal.*

*Through the support of my family, my doctor, and my friends, things began to improve. I still have some moments where I slip down in the tunnel, but I recognize it most of the time and can get traction and get back up. I use the analogy that life is like a cup of water. Everyday life/stress drips into the cup, and it begins to fill up. I used to suppress all my events. You know? "Suck it up" and put it in the back of my brain somewhere. Be the tough cop and work through it. Well, this caused my cup to overflow, and I began changing emotionally, mentally, and physically. I would become frustrated, angry, and/or overwhelmed. I have learned to manage the 'dripping' so my cup doesn't overflow as often. I am still learning and managing, but I am so much better than I was.*

*I am now able to recognize many of my triggers and have changed my life so I can either avoid the trigger or manage it. My goal is to be able to go to crowded rooms and not get overwhelmed, watch the movies I want, meet new people, and become the person I used to be but better.*

*I felt I needed to tell my story to let people suffering know that YOU ARE NOT ALONE. You are not going crazy. Because of the trauma you have witnessed or been involved with, whether direct or indirect, you have changed. You are reacting normally to abnormal events. TALKING HELPS. There is help available. Go to your Human Resources department, talk to someone in your Peer-to-Peer support or CISM Unit, see your doctor, and/or talk to a friend. Many people out there have gone through what you are going through and have learned how to manage it to the point that they are back from going down that tunnel.*

*As the now retired Abbotsford Police Chief Constable Bob Rich said, "Take a knee." Many people in the same boat have taken that knee, got the help, regained the control in their life, and have maintained their career or have even moved up. So, don't let the stigma get in the way. You don't need to stand on a soap box and announce to the world, but you don't have to hide it either. I am one example of many, so please, reach out, and get help.*

*Thanks for reading. I hope it helps.*

# CHAPTER 3

## DEPRESSION

Depression is a mood disorder characterized by an ongoing feeling of sadness and hopelessness. Bipolar and unipolar depression are the two major types of mood disorder experienced by most individuals across the globe. Around 17 percent of adults in the world experience an episode of unipolar depression at some point in their lives. The onset of unipolar depression is caused by traumatic and stressful events, such as loss of a loved one and lack of employment. Depression is among the most commonly known mental illnesses in the world and yet only a few individuals can tell what exactly it is. Depression is a symptom of a clear reluctance and the lack of will to live, which makes most individuals end up self-harming through drinking alcohol, cutting themselves, using illegal drugs, or even committing suicide (Kendall-Tackett, 2016).

A person who is in a state of depression loses his motivation and energy to function normally in daily life. Stress and anxiety lead to depression, and it is very significant for an individual to seek medical attention early, as medical professionals can detect signs and symptoms of this mental disorder and determine if they are depressed or not.

The word "depression" can sometimes be misleading, because people use it on a daily basis to describe a temporary depressing feeling that does not often reflect a clinical problem. Temporary feelings of sadness and depression are normal, and healthcare professionals refer to them as a natural part of our lives, caused by unpleasant events and negative internal feelings. When a person is experiencing clinical depression, those feelings go beyond any reason or proportion to external causes. All the life events we experience may bring happiness or sadness. People who are faced with difficult situations, which may leave them depressed, need counselling, so that they can cope with these situations and continue working and living with some normality.

CHAPTER 3: DEPRESSION

## Signs and Symptoms of Depression

Being unhappy is not the same as being depressed. Depression is a term used to loosely describe how someone feels after a bad week at work, or when they are going through a breakup. However, a major depressive disorder, which is a type of depression, is much more complicated. There are certain signs and symptoms used by healthcare professionals to determine whether a person is depressed or are just experiencing normal sadness from daily activities they engage in. However, determining if persistent, unshakable dark feelings are the result of depression is the first step used towards the recovery process. A person who is depressed may experience the following signs and symptoms (Segal, Williams & Teasdale, 2018):

They may experience a hopeless outlook. Depression is a cruel mental illness, which can affect any person, but is very easy to manage if the signs are recognized early in advance. Major depression is described as a mood disorder that can affect the way we feel about life in general. Having a hopeless and helpless outlook on your life is the most common sign of depression. A person who is depressed may also feel worthless, self-hatred, and inappropriate guilt.

Another symptom of depression is lost interest. A person who has lost interest may feel more negative about going to a job. This is because depression takes the pleasures or enjoyment out of the things someone loves, making a person lose interest and withdraw from activities he/she once loved, like sports, hobbies, and going out with friends. A person may also experience decreased sex drive and even become impotent. Increased fatigue and sleeping problems are also another sign associated with someone who is experiencing anxiety, stress, and depression. Among the main reasons that make a depressed person stop doing the things they enjoy is fatigue (Gilbert, 2016). Depression is accompanied by lack of energy and an overwhelming feeling of tiredness, which are known to be among the most debilitating symptoms of depression. This leads to excessive sleeping.

Anxiety is another main sign of depression. Though there is not enough proof to conclude that anxiety causes depression, the two conditions occur together. A person experiencing anxiety may be nervous, restless, and tensed. They may also feel in danger, panicky, and dread. The last sign and symptom of depression is a change in appetite and weight. Weight and appetite of people with depression change greatly. Some may experience increased appetite leading to weight gain, while others will not feel hungry and thus lose weight. An indication of whether dietary changes are related to depression is whether they are intentional or not. If they are, it may mean they are caused by depression.

### You're Not Stuck

---

You're just committed to certain patterns of behaviour because they

helped you in the past. Now those behaviours have become

more harmful than helpful. The reason why you can't move

forward is because you keep applying an old principle to a new

level in your life. Change the principle to get a different result.

## Why Depression Leads to Self-Harm

Self-harm is defined as a condition when someone wants to hurt or harm himself/herself on purpose. Self-harm is not a mental problem, but it can be a sign of a mental disorder. Healthcare professionals associate self-harm with mental disorders like depression. There are several ways in which people self-harm, and these include cutting, burning, breaking bones, and hair pulling or picking skin. Self-harm can also include taking illegal drugs and drinking alcohol too much to harm yourself (Hysing, Stormark & O'Connor, 2015). For depressed people, this is much different from normal drinking and the taking of drugs for pleasure. People take toxic substances so that they may feel better afterward, which can have serious impacts on your health. Most individuals who think of self-harm and try to take their own life usually want to end the pain they are going through in their life completely. Most depressed individuals try to self-harm so that they can feel better. Self-harm is considered a sign of stress, anxiety, and depression. Self-harm enables most depressed people to try and work out what the problem is, which means they end up getting the right help and treatment. Talking about self-harm is stressful and brings up a lot of emotions.

However, depressed people should be encouraged, so that they do not engage themselves in activities that can negatively affect their health. There are many reasons why people experiencing stress, anxiety, and depression opt to self-harm. According to various studies, people self-harm for different reasons. These reasons can be grouped into three categories:

The first is **"Controlling Moods."** This happens because most people find it hard to cope with emotions and feelings, especially feelings that are unsettling, unpleasant, and strong. Depressed people who end up self-harming find it hard to deal with these sorts of emotions. Self-harm takes away these emotions, making a depressed person feel relieved.

The second category is **"Communication."** Most depressed people tend to self-harm so that they can communicate what they are feeling. However, some people see this as a form of attention seeking, and thus ignore them (Kim et al., 2015).

The last is "Control." Depressed people self-harm as a form of gaining some control. This is because they feel like they don't have control over their life, which makes them frightened. Studies indicate that around one in ten people who self-harm will do it again within a year. Therefore, it is significant for people who self-harm to seek medical attention and support, because they are at risk of doing it again.

Self-harming does not always mean someone wants to end their life. Most people do it just to communicate what they feel with others, trying to feel better, and to punish themselves for a mistake they made, which is stressing. However, for example, if someone cuts himself/herself and there is no one around to help them, they may bleed until they die.

## I am Depression.

---

I'm the emptiness you feel at two a.m., the tears with no meaning,

the pain when you smile. I don't come alone. I bring my closest friends.

We are the scars that cover your body, the voice that you despise, but soon learn to trust.

I'm the only thing you will feel. Me

I am Depression.

## Effects of Self-Harm

Impacts of self-harm—also known as self-injury and self-mutilation—are varied, and they are both physical and psychological. Though the physical effects of self-harm are obvious and harmful, the psychological impacts of self-harm are no less damaging. Physical impacts of self-harm can be minor, such as a scratch or small bruise, but in rare cases, they are life-threatening. No matter how severe they are, physical effects of self-injury indicate the unmanageable pain a person is in, and the severity of the injury shows the severity of the pain. Most individuals who self-harm do it more than once, and some physical signs of self-harm include wounds or scars on the skin. They may also experience infections as a result of their open wounds meeting germs. Some people experiencing stress, anxiety, and depression self-harm by pulling their hair, which means hair loss and bald spots can be a sign of someone who is exercising self-harm.

Just because people do not see the psychological effects of self-harm does not mean they are not happening. Not only do they cause strong feelings but they also tend to drive people to do it repeatedly. Some psychological effects of self-injury are irritability (Hawton et al., 2016). Depressed people who are self-harming have a great desire to be alone, in order to practice it or to hide evidence that they are doing it. These people are always ashamed and guilty due to stress and the difficulty of having to lie to those around them. Depressed people practicing this malicious act have low self-esteem and self-hatred, and they feel like they cannot do anything good on their own, which makes the situation worse.

Depression is a common mental disorder affecting people across the globe. This disorder is brought up by a stressful condition behold our control. Life experiences that cause depression include the loss of your loved one. Most depressed people tend to relieve the pain they are experiencing by self-harming through drinking alcohol or taking illicit drugs, and even cutting themselves. However, this is not the solution, and they should be advised to seek medical attention so that they can be helped by healthcare professionals.

## You Got 'Em

FLAWS, I got 'em

LAWS, I broke 'em

DUES, I paid 'em

SCARS, I bear 'em

LESSONS, I learned 'em

PROBLEMS, I still have 'em

That's life. I still love it

## The Sad Thing

---

The sad thing is nobody ever really knows

How much anyone else is hurting.

We could be standing next to somebody who is

Completely broken, and we would not even know.

# CHAPTER 3: DEPRESSION

## Story Shared by Author
## When You Think This is the Last Day

*It was an early rise in Camp Butmir. Rise and shine was usually about 0530. Today was a different day, as we were heading out on a TAV (technical assistance visit) to Dubrovnik, Croatia. The detachment deployed there was in dire need of a communication upgrade to their infrastructure, so basically this was a visit to see their needs, and what material and resources would be needed.*

*As like any other day, my feet hit the floor, and I grabbed my socks, then my combat pants and my old worn lineman boots. As usual, I grabbed my pistol and strapped her on like any other day, not knowing she would be utilized later that day. As I finished dressing, I put the final touches on my 'go bag'.*

*So off to breakfast we go. This was a challenge. To put it in perspective, we had 1,300 soldiers from 32 different nations eating out of the same chow hall, so the common breakfast wasn't so common. After breakfast, we went over to the SSG (Signal Support Group) Line Team Head Quarters. We met up with the LTC (Line Team Chief) and received our orders, which included the ROE (Rules of Engagement), which were that any NATO (North Atlantic Treaty Organization) vehicles were not to stopped or detained by any military or civilian entities. With a final wave to the LTC, we were off and with our orders. We would check in when we arrived Dubrovnik.*

*The TAV crew consisted of a MCpl. (leader), Cpl. (driver), US Marine (wire dawg), and a US Sgt who was also a lineman. As you can tell, our SSG team was extremely diverse. On the way out of camp, we briefly stopped by the barracks and grabbed the 'go bags', and then out the front gate, with our usual thumbs up to the security, which was manned by the Turks.*

*The trip is 235 kms. With the normal driving conditions, this would be approximately a four-hour drive; however, this day it was close to eight hours. It was 140 kms to the Bosnian and Croatian border. These roads were filled with minefields and local farmers with their goats, sheep, and cows. The local vendors would sell meat (goat) on a spit to passing people, and the drink of choice was a local concoction of fruits, which was fermented into Slivovitz (moonshine).*

*As we approached the border, the traffic was backed up for kilometers. Seeing this and remembering the ROEs, I directed the corporal to pull left and proceed slowly in the left lane. My hands were sweating, and my heart was pounding so hard that I was sure you could see my shirt move.*

*I would say we were about one kilometre from the border crossing, and the guard raised his rifle, which looked like an AK-47. He was fixed and frozen on us like a statue. I directed the crew to pull their pistols out, take the safeties off, and put them out the window pointed at the guard, and told them not to fire until I gave the order. At that moment, I thought I was not coming home. This was it. We were about twenty-five metres from the guard, and he lowered his rifle and started laughing extremely loud at us. Then I knew he was messing with us. Nonetheless, this was the first time in my life I thought I was a 'goner'. I told the crew to put the pistols back on safety and re-holster them. It was extremely quiet the rest of the drive.*

*A few hours later, we arrived in Dubrovnik, checked in with the Detachment and LTC, and reported what we experienced with our near miss. We finally arrived at the barracks, dropped our bags, and directly went and had a cigarette and a well-deserved cold beverage.*

## I Don't Care

I don't care who you are

What you look like or

How you choose to live your life.

If you are good to me, I will be good to you.

# CHAPTER 4

# SEASON AFFECTIVE DISORDER (SAD)

Seasonal affective disorder (SAD) is a type of depression that's related to changes in seasons. SAD begins and ends at about the same time every year. If you're like most people with SAD, your symptoms start in the fall and continue into the winter months, sapping your energy and making you feel moody. Less often, SAD causes depression in the spring or early summer. Wikipedia 2019 has stated that Seasonal affective disorder (SAD) is a mood disorder subset in which people who have normal mental health throughout most of the year exhibit depressive symptoms at the same time each year, most commonly in the winter. (Ivry, 2002) Common symptoms include sleeping too much, having little to no energy, and overeating. Wikipedia 2019 has stated "The condition in the summer can include heightened anxiety."

Treatment for SAD may include light therapy (phototherapy), medications, and psychotherapy.

Don't brush off that yearly feeling as simply a case of the "winter blues" or a seasonal funk that you must tough out on your own. Take steps to keep your mood and motivation steady throughout the year.

## Symptoms of SAD

In most cases, seasonal affective disorder symptoms appear during late fall or early winter and go away during the sunnier days of spring and summer. Less commonly, people with the opposite pattern have symptoms that begin in spring or summer. In either case, symptoms may start out mild and become more severe as the season progresses. (Mayo Clinic, 2018)

# CHAPTER 4: SEASON AFFECTIVE DISORDER (SAD)

<u>Signs and symptoms of SAD may include:</u>

- Feeling depressed most of the day, nearly every day
- Losing interest in activities you once enjoyed
- Having low energy
- Having problems with sleeping
- Experiencing changes in your appetite or weight
- Feeling sluggish or agitated
- Having difficulty concentrating
- Feeling hopeless, worthless, or guilty
- Having frequent thoughts of death or suicide

Even with a thorough evaluation, it can sometimes be difficult for your doctor or mental-health professional to diagnose seasonal affective disorder because other types of depression or other mental-health conditions can cause similar symptoms. To help diagnose SAD, your doctor or mental-health professional may do a thorough evaluation, which generally includes:

- Physical exam. Your doctor may do a physical exam and ask in-depth questions about your health. In some cases, depression may be linked to an underlying physical-health problem.
- Lab tests. For example, your doctor may do a blood test called a "complete blood count" (CBC) or test your thyroid to make sure it's functioning properly.
- Psychological evaluation. To check for signs of depression, your doctor or mental-health professional asks about your symptoms, thoughts, feelings, and behaviour patterns. You may fill out a questionnaire to help answer these questions.
- DSM-5. Your mental-health professional may use the criteria for seasonal depressive episodes listed in the *Diagnostic and Statistical Manual of Mental Disorders (DSM-5),* published by the American Psychiatric Association.

## Treatment of SAD

Treatment for Seasonal Affective Disorder may include light therapy, medications, and psychotherapy. If you have bipolar disorder, tell your doctor. This is critical to know when prescribing light therapy or an antidepressant. Both treatments can potentially trigger a manic episode.

### I Embrace Change

---

Change is the only constant in life.

I embrace this truth as a beautiful thing.

I embrace endings, for they give birth to new beginnings…

For every dusk brings a new dawn.

I embrace beginnings, for they are rich in hope and possibility…

For every idea was once only imagined.

I embrace change, for it promises new life and a chance to begin again…

For there is no other way that life could be.

I live in this circle of life, infinitely and happily…

For I dwell in the present moment, the one eternal gift of this life.

Aimhappy.com

CHAPTER 4: SEASON AFFECTIVE DISORDER (SAD)

# Light Therapy for SAD

In light therapy, also called phototherapy, you sit a few feet from a special light box so that you're exposed to bright light within the first hour of waking up each day. Light therapy mimics natural outdoor light and appears to cause a change in brain chemicals linked to mood.

Light therapy is one of the first-line treatments for fall-onset SAD. It generally starts working in a few days to a few weeks and causes few side effects. Research on light therapy is limited, but it appears to be effective for most people in relieving SAD symptoms.

Before you purchase a light box, talk with your doctor about the best one for you, and familiarize yourself with the variety of features and options, so that you buy a high-quality product that's safe and effective. Also ask your doctor about how and when to use the light box.

Some people with SAD benefit from antidepressant treatment, especially if symptoms are severe. An extended-release version of the antidepressant bupropion (Wellbutrin XL, Aplenzin) may help prevent depressive episodes in people with a history of SAD. Other antidepressants also may commonly be used to treat SAD.

Your doctor may recommend starting treatment with an antidepressant before your symptoms typically begin each year. He or she may also recommend that you continue to take the antidepressant beyond the time your symptoms normally go away.

Keep in mind that it may take several weeks to notice full benefits from an antidepressant. In addition, you may have to try different medications before you find one that works well for you and has the fewest side effects.

## Psychotherapy for SAD

Psychotherapy, also called talk therapy, is another option to treat SAD. A type of psychotherapy known as cognitive behavioural therapy can help you:

- Identify and change negative thoughts and behaviours that may be making you feel worse
- Learn healthy ways to cope with SAD, especially with reducing avoidance behaviour and scheduling activities
- Learn how to manage stress

## Mind-body Connection for SAD

Examples of mind-body techniques that some people may choose to try to help cope with SAD include:

- Relaxation techniques such as yoga or tai chi
- Meditation
- Guided imagery
- Music or art therapy

## History of SAD

SAD was first systematically reported and named in the early 1980s by Norman E. Rosenthal, M.D., and his associates at the National Institute of Mental Health (NIMH). Rosenthal was initially motivated by his desire to discover the cause of his own experience of depression during the dark days of the Northern US winter. He theorized that the reduction in available natural light during winter was the cause. Rosenthal and his colleagues then documented the phenomenon of SAD in a placebo-controlled study utilizing light therapy. (Rosenthal et al, 1984). Although Rosenthal's ideas were initially greeted with skepticism, SAD has become well recognized, and his 1993 book has become the standard introduction to the subject.

CHAPTER 4: SEASON AFFECTIVE DISORDER (SAD)

Research on SAD in the United States began in 1979, when Herb Kern, a research engineer, had also noticed that he felt depressed during the winter months. Kern suspected that scarcer light in winter was the cause and discussed the idea with scientists at the NIMH, who were working on bodily rhythms. They were intrigued and responded by devising a lightbox to treat Kern's depression. Kern felt much better within a few days of treatments, as did other patients treated in the same way.

It has also been suggested that SAD affects risky behaviour, and those affected by SAD are more likely to opt for conservative investments, whether financially or scientifically.

## Lifestyle methods to cope with Seasonal Affective Disorder

### Plan a Trip

For people living in more northern areas that have drastic changes in weather like snow, rain, and freezing temperatures, sometimes you just need to break up the dark months with a trip to somewhere hot. If possible, go on a trip down south to get a week of sunshine and warm weather, something that will lift your spirits while getting an enviable tan. On top of the short burst of heat, planning a trip also gives you something to look forward to. Counting down the days until you get several relaxing, warm days of sunshine is a great motivator and way to improve your mood.

### Make Social Plans

It can be tempting to plop yourself on your couch and watch endless hours of TV when you're experiencing Seasonal Affective Disorder, but doing so will only make things worse. Instead of hibernating, make plans with friends and family. Get out of the house at least once a week, if not more. Even meeting a friend for a cup of coffee could lift your spirits. Going out could also help you adjust better to the fall and winter months, and make things feel a little less doom and gloom by preventing the seasonal changes from affecting your social life.

### Soak Up the Sun as Often as Possible

While you may not enjoy the cold weather, odds are there are quite a few days during the fall and winter months that you can layer up and spend time outside. The sun might not be around for as long as you'd like, but going outside and soaking up the rays whenever you can could help reduce your symptoms of seasonal affective disorder. Our bodies crave sunlight, so instead of cooping up in your house for five or six months, bundle up and head outside. Who knows? You might even learn to appreciate the cooler temperatures!

### Avoid Overloading on Carbs

During the winter, you're likely to turn to comfort foods filled with carbohydrates that sit heavily in your stomach. Pastas and breads, mashed potatoes and pies can tempt you to overload on carbs. While it isn't necessary to cut out carbs completely from your diet, having too much can worsen your symptoms of seasonal affective disorder. Carbs can make you cathartic, directly affecting your mood with the spike and inevitable drop in your glucose level. Instead, eat a healthy, balanced diet rich in fruit, vegetables, protein, and fiber. Get as much of the good stuff as you can and cut back on the carbs if you're feeling sleepy and lazy a lot throughout the winter.

### Make Room For 'Me Time'

Me time isn't just about being alone; it's a time for you to be selfish (because you deserve it) and do something that you want to do. Read a book, take a bath, rent a movie, get a pedicure, try a new recipe… It simply doesn't matter what you enjoy, if you do it. Take the opportunity to do something that makes you happy and gives you something to look forward to. Try getting this well-deserved time to yourself at least once a week. The weather is often a deterrent to following through on plans, but don't let that get in your way. Push yourself to have your 'me time' and don't make excuses.

## Exercise Regularly

It seems that almost every health issue can be helped by making sure you exercise regularly, and it's easy to understand why. While regular exercise is improving your physical health, it can also greatly improve your mood during the cold winter months. When you exercise, endorphins are released into your body, bringing forth positive feelings and increasing your energy. You'll also reap the benefits of regular exercise: increasing your strength, cutting down your body fat, and feeling good and healthy overall. And of course, couple regular exercise with eating well, and your whole body will feel better.

## Consider Seeing a Therapist

Seasonal affective disorder is a form of depression, and sometimes the best treatment is talking it out with a therapist or using a combination of therapy and lifestyle changes. If you experience moderate to severe winter depression, meaning it affects several areas of your life and prevents you from doing things, seeing a therapist could help. Sometimes small lifestyle changes are enough to pick someone up when they're feeling low, but it doesn't work for everyone. Seeing a therapist can get you to address negative feelings and learn how to change your perspective and behaviour accordingly. It may also help prevent you from falling into the same cycle in the years to come.

## Let the Light In

One of the easiest ways to help cope with your winter depression is to let daylight into your house wherever and whenever you can. It's common to close your drapes and blinds during the winter, because of the cold weather and fewer hours of sun, but uncovering your windows to let natural daylight shine through could give you the mood boost you need to get out of your funk. Sit near windows when you can, and don't close your drapes until the evening. Accepting and embracing the daylight you're given can help you get past some of the symptoms you experience from seasonal affective disorder.

### Light Box Therapy

Light box therapy is a popular and often very effective way to cope with mild seasonal affective disorder. They're effective, because they mimic the sun's rays. You should use the light box every day in the morning to get the most benefit from it, and you can turn it on while you do normal tasks, like talking on the phone, eating breakfast, or working. Doctors differ in opinion on how many hours you should be exposed to light boxes, and like any form of depression, what works for one person might not work for another. Talk to your doctor to see where you should start.

### Take Medication If Needed

There are so many different symptoms of seasonal affective disorder, and the severity in which you experience these symptoms differs from person to person. In some cases, you'll need to add medication as part of your treatment plan to effectively cope with the winter blues. If you're struggling with SAD, and it's affecting your daily activities or your relationships, your doctor may suggest an antidepressant to help you get through it. Talk to your doctor about the different options available. In some cases, vitamin supplements could also be recommended to go along with other medications and coping techniques.

## Story Share by Anonymous
## Living With SAD

*Even though I live in the south, winters can be brutal on my body, mental health, and self-image. I have finally come to terms with the fact that I have seasonal affective disorder (SAD), a disorder that saps my energy and mood, beginning with the weather changes in fall and into winter. When my friends and family ask me to attend any events in the winter, and I refuse to go, it's not because I am*

## CHAPTER 4: SEASON AFFECTIVE DISORDER (SAD)

*antisocial; it's because my body is aching, my mind is foggy, and I am tired. SAD does this to me every year, even after light therapy and changes in my diet.*

*My body feels heavy, bloated, and I lose all feeling in my hands and legs throughout the day. My feet hurt and are frozen most days. I pile my body inside comforters, blankets, and soft pillows for relief. Most days, I sleep until noon, making it impossible to be productive in my full-time job. I crave sunlight; however, I am much too tired and sick to go for my usual walk, and when I do, I am unable to walk very far. My mood with SAD leaves me in a perpetual fog. It's akin to having a heavy, dim cloud follow you around every day, weighing on your back. Even though I try to have a healthy diet, my body craves carbohydrates and fats, and it's all I can do to just grab something hot and easy to prepare. The pain, extreme fatigue, and lack of energy cause winter weight gain, and my body feels like a zombie for much of the winter months. Having SAD makes me guilty, and I feel lonely from the isolation.*

*So, why don't I smile in the winter? It's because I am melancholy, and SAD lives up to its name. There are times when the weather is extremely cold, and if I bear to brave going outside, I sit in my car with the heat blaring for hours, unable to walk inside stores or work. I fear I won't be able to make my way in the world and that people will think I am lazy. Yet, I haven't been able to rearrange my life to fit into the will of the disorder, although the disorder takes over any will I have to be creative. For many months, I thought my light therapy was working, but after a while, I noticed that, even if I got out of bed after a few hours, I was back into the sunken place of depression and zapped with body pain.*

## Story Share by Anonymous
## A Man's SAD Story

"It felt like somebody boosted my battery." This man is talking about a winter vacation to Mexico, where the strong sunlight gave him a physical and mental lift that lasted for months back home.

The family physician from Calgary, where winter can seemingly span half the year, had observed that his mood regularly fell as temperatures started to dip. Come spring and summer, his zest for life would return.

*Despite his medical background, however, it would be years before he accepted that he has seasonal affective disorder, or SAD. This type of depression arises when seasonal changes in sunlight levels affect brain chemistry.*

*After doing some research when he was finally diagnosed, he realized that he was not alone in shrugging off the symptoms associated with SAD.*

*"SAD seems to be the poor cousin of depression," he says. "Even though it might not feel so good, life goes on and you get better in a couple of months. There are reprieves. But it can be as severe as other forms of depression and should not be pushed into a corner or dismissed."*

*He came to another conclusion: "It was really important to get that message out to the medical community." And he was just the guy to do it.*

*A runner and cyclist, he channeled those passions into the SAD No More Canadian Tour 2010. The awareness campaign, which took him from the lush island of Victoria in British Columbia to the lunar coast of Newfoundland, included thirty-five formal presentations to medical professionals, as well as numerous media interviews.*

*The tour lasted from August through October, the month Jablonski's depression typically kicks in. The early signs can be unsettling.*

*"It's almost a feeling of dread," he says, "as if you have something looming on the horizon that you aren't happy about, that feeling in the pit of your stomach."*

*Over the next six months or so, he doesn't sleep as well. He starts obsessing about little things. He notices that his usual sharp wits start to lose their edge. He has less energy, craves more coffee and junk food for stimulation, and gains weight.*

*He ignored his annual symptoms, if he was able to do well at his doctoring duties. He says he has missed only two days of work, both for surgeries, in twenty-five years of practice. The seasonal nature of his symptoms helped carry him through.*

*"All I needed was a few more months," he explains. He became "absolutely miserable, irritable, and completely unable to enjoy myself," he recalls.*

*"Much to the dismay of my wife, I begged her to leave early from an absolutely exquisite dinner and spent the rest of the evening on my hotel bed, staring at the ceiling with feelings of complete and utter worthlessness. I thought, 'What's the point of living?'*

*"That's when I accepted the facts and decided to seek treatment. Up until then, there was no way in hell that I would admit to anything. I could get*

by in my personal life. But when it impacted my professional life, that's when things changed."

He was diagnosed with SAD within weeks.

During bouts of severe depression, typically brought on by increased stress, he resorts to antidepressants. Daily, he relies on light therapy, also known as phototherapy. Exposure to bright artificial light that mimics the spectrum and intensity of the summer sun is thought to ease SAD symptoms. As the light indirectly strikes the retina of the eye, it stimulates chemical changes in the brain that lift mood.

The process also seems to reset the body's natural circadian rhythm, or internal clock, which governs sleep cycles, hormone production, and other biological functions.

Phototherapy helps him sleep better not only because of its physiological effects but also because his regimen keeps him on a regular sleep schedule. He gets up at six a.m. to spend time in front of a device called a light therapy box, tricking his brain into thinking it's a summer day when the sun rises early. He uses a smaller, portable light box if he's on the treadmill or exercise bike.

"It's tough on a cold winter day when I'd rather be lying in a nice warm bed, but it's critical that I get up early and do light therapy," he says. "I can't uncouple those two."

On the professional side, he says, he has become "much more sophisticated" in diagnosing depression and probing to discover whether a patient's moods change with the seasons.

He hopes his cross-country tour inspired other physicians to dig a little deeper when dealing with a patient whose symptoms appear transitory.

"I think people in the medical community are a little more aware of SAD now," he says. "My dream was for this to have some life afterward, to keep the message going, and I'm still being asked to speak. So, it still has legs."

# CHAPTER 5

## ADDICTION

Addiction is a brain disorder characterized by compulsive engagement in rewarding stimuli despite adverse consequences. Despite the involvement of several psychosocial factors, a biological process—one which is induced by repeated exposure to an addictive stimulus—is the core pathology that drives the development and maintenance of an addiction. The two properties that characterize all addictive stimuli are that they are reinforcing (i.e., they increase the likelihood that a person will seek repeated exposure to them) and intrinsically rewarding (i.e., they are perceived as being inherently positive, desirable, and pleasurable).

Addiction is a psychological and physical inability to stop consuming a chemical, drug activity, or substance, even though it is causing psychological and physical harm.

The term "addiction" does not only refer to dependence on substances such as heroin or cocaine. A person who cannot stop taking a drug or chemical has a substance dependence.

Some addictions also involve an inability to stop partaking in activities, such as gambling, eating, or working. In these circumstances, a person has a behavioural addiction.

Addiction is a chronic disease that can also result from taking medications. According to a publication by the Health Officers Council, there were 47,000 deaths yearly in Canada. When a person experiences addiction, they cannot control how they use a substance or partake in an activity, and they become dependent on it to cope with daily life.

Every year, addiction to alcohol, tobacco, illicit drugs, and prescription opioids costs Canada economy upward of **$200 billion** in treatment costs, lost work, and the effects of crime. Most people start using a drug or first engage in an activity voluntarily. However, addiction can take over and reduce self-control.

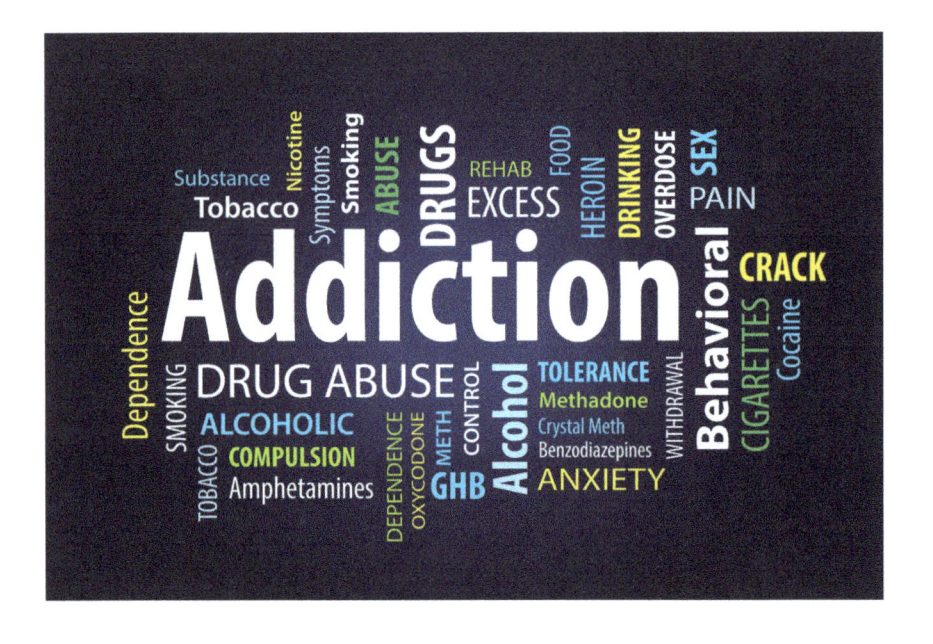

CHAPTER 5: ADDICTION

## Addiction vs. Misuse

Not everyone that misuses a substance has an addiction.

Drug addiction and drug misuse are different.

Misuse refers to the incorrect, excessive, or non-therapeutic use of body and mind-altering substances. However, not everybody that misuses a substance has an addiction. Addiction is the long-term inability to moderate or cease intake. For example, a person who drinks alcohol heavily on a night out may experience both the euphoric and harmful effects of the substance.

However, this does not qualify as an addiction until the person feels the need to consume this amount of alcohol regularly, alone, or at times of day when the alcohol will likely impair regular activities, such as in the morning.

### My Bout with Addiction

---

Coming back from drug and alcohol addiction is one of the hardest things you'll ever do.

It will hurt. It will take time.

You'll have to rebuild your entire life from scratch.

You'll have to figure out how to live life on life's terms.

You'll have to find the strength within you, because nobody can do it for you.

Don't ever lose faith and hope.

Recovery is possible.

A person who has not yet developed an addiction may be put off further use by the harmful side effects of substance abuse. For example, vomiting or waking up with a hangover after drinking too much alcohol may deter some people from drinking that amount anytime soon. Someone with an addiction will continue to misuse the substance despite the harmful effects.

## Symptoms of Addiction

The primary indications of addiction are:

- uncontrollably seeking drugs
- uncontrollably engaging in harmful levels of habit-forming behaviour
- neglecting or losing interest in activities that do not involve the harmful substance or behaviour
- relationship difficulties, which often involve lashing out at people who identify the dependency
- an inability to stop using a drug, though it may be causing health problems or personal problems, such as issues with employment or relationships
- hiding substances or behaviours and otherwise exercising secrecy, for example, by refusing to explain injuries that occurred while under the influence
- profound changes in appearance, including a noticeable abandonment of hygiene
- increased risk-taking, both to access the substance or activity and while using it or engaging in it.

Millions of Canadians struggle with some form of addiction. If you are one of them, know that you are not alone, and that many treatment options exist to help you overcome your addiction.

*Polydrug Use*

Most people who seek treatment for a substance-use disorder are struggling with a dependence on more than one type of substance. Polydrug use involves the consumption of one type of substance with another. This is often done to intensify the effects of a certain drug or achieve a stronger high. In some cases, a person may take a stimulant, such as Adderall, to counteract the sedative effects of an opioid such as oxycodone. However, mixing multiple types of drugs together is extremely dangerous, and can potentially lead to overdose and death.

## The Top 10 Most Common Addictions

Millions of people around the world struggle with substance abuse. Some of the most common drugs that impede people's lives include:

- Nicotine
- Alcohol
- Cocaine
- Heroin
- Cigarettes
- And more.

Stopping the use of a drug can lead to anxiety. When a person has an addiction, and they stop taking the substance or engaging in the behaviour, they may experience certain symptoms.

These symptoms include:

- anxiety
- Irritability
- tremors and shaking
- nausea
- vomiting
- fatigue
- a loss of appetite

If a person has regularly used alcohol or benzodiazepines, and they stop suddenly or without medical supervision, withdrawal can be fatal.

## Treatments of Addiction

Support groups and rehabilitation programs can be vital to recovery. Medicinal advances and progress in diagnosing have helped the medical community develop various ways to manage and resolve addiction.

Methods include:

- behavioural therapy and counseling
- medication and drug-based treatment
- medical devices to treat withdrawal
- treating related psychological factors, such as depression
- ongoing care to reduce the risk of relapse

Addiction treatment is highly personalized and often requires the support of the individual's community or family. Treatment can take a long time and may be complicated. Addiction is a chronic condition with a range of psychological and physical effects. Each substance or behaviour may require different management.

Addiction is a serious, chronic dependence on a substance or activity. The prevalence of addiction costs the U.S. economy hundreds of billions of dollars every year. A person with an addiction is unable to stop taking a substance or engaging in a behaviour, though it has harmful effects on daily living.

Misuse is different from addiction. Substance misuse does not always lead to addiction, while addiction involves regular misuse of substances or engagement in harmful behaviour. Symptoms of addiction often include declining physical health, irritation, fatigue, and an inability to cease using a substance or engaging in a behaviour. Addiction can lead to behaviour that strains relationships and inhibits daily activities.

Ceasing to use the substance or engage in the behaviour often leads to withdrawal symptoms, including nausea and shaking. Do not attempt to suddenly stop using alcohol or benzodiazepines without medical supervision. Addiction treatment can be difficult, but it is effective. The best form of treatment depends on the substance and the presentation of the addiction, which varies from person to person. However, treatment often involves counseling, medication, and community support

## The Cost of Addiction

Addiction is notable for the toll it takes on an individual's health and relationships. However, while these losses feature prominently in the costs of addiction, they only tell part of the story. Typically, addicts and their families also pay a heavy financial cost, both in terms of the money spent on the substance or activity in question and in terms of lost wages and job opportunities. Society also pays a significant cost due to factors such as lost productivity, healthcare expenses for indigent addicts, drug-treatment programs, drug-related law-enforcement efforts, and the housing of drug offenders in jails and prisons.

## Addiction Expenditures

An alcoholic who drinks a twelve-pack of beer each day spends about $26 dollars a day to support his/her addiction. This same rate of consumption produces costs of roughly $182 per week, $728 per month, and a total of $8,736 per year. A nicotine addict who smokes only a pack a day can spend roughly $5,800 a year on cigarettes. People with heavy nicotine habits can bear costs that reach or exceed about $10,000 per year. While it's more difficult to accurately estimate the cost of addiction to illegal drugs, conservative estimates indicate that a marijuana user can spend close to $4,000 a year, while a methamphetamine addict can spend $9,000 or more each year. People addicted to cocaine or heroin can easily spend $15,000 or more per year to support their habits. A person with a gambling addiction can easily financially ruin him/herself and any unfortunate family members.

## Loss of Income and Productivity

People addicted to drugs or alcohol frequently experience problems at work that endanger their jobs or simply reduce their ability to act as valuable employees. Substance addicts and abusers also miss work relatively frequently and miss out on promotions that could improve their financial status. In addition, addicts and abusers typically have a lower educational standing than other members of the workforce from similar social backgrounds. Over a lifetime, the income lost from dropping out of school or failing to gain an advanced education can add up to literally tens or hundreds of thousands of dollars—sometimes even more in extreme cases.

## Bills and Insurance Costs

Over time, long-term addicts inevitably develop health problems that can cost them significant amounts of money in the form of either direct expenditures or increased health insurance premiums. These same health problems also typically cause a significant loss of work-related income. On average, addicts and alcoholics are subject to 1.4 DUI stops over the course of their lifetimes, and thus see increases in their car insurance premiums that can rise as high as 300 percent. Some people bear even heavier burdens when insurance companies cancel their policies.

## Social Costs

Periodically, the National Institute on Drug Abuse (NIDA) and the Surgeon General's office release reports that attempt to estimate the overall social costs of substance abuse and addiction. The latest of these reports, which dates to 2004, estimates that illegal drug use costs society $181 billion each year in combined expenditures for healthcare, enforcement of drug laws, crimes committed by addicts and abusers, lost productivity, and jail and prison facilities for drug offenders. According to this same report, alcohol abuse and addiction have a social cost of roughly $185 billion each year, while tobacco addiction has a social cost of roughly $193 billion a year. When combined, the costs for these three categories of use equal about $559 billion per year.

## Disproportionate Impact on Lower Income Families

Addiction has a disproportionately heavy cost in low-income households, where budgets rarely allow for any form of lost income. At the poverty level, Forbes explains, even a one-pack-a-day cigarette habit can consume fully 10 percent of a family's entire monthly budget. Users of hardcore drugs can easily spend more than half of their available income supporting their habits. Addiction can also help trap future generations of a family in a cycle of poverty. For instance, many children of substance abusers or addicts strive to emulate their parents' behaviour and either develop addictive relationships to the same substances or develop similar relationships to a different substance. In poor families, this adoption of parents' behaviour can also include emulation of inadequate money-management skills, lack of an adequate education, and lack of access to the opportunities that typically come with higher income and a higher educational status.

## Physical Complications

Overdosing can lead to a life-threatening medical emergency. Overusing mood or physiology-altering substances can cause damage in several ways.

**Direct effects of substances:** For example, snorting cocaine through the nose can damage nasal cartilage, and taking opiates can lead to opiate-induced constipation, a chronic and potentially fatal form of constipation, if a person does not receive treatment.

Felman (2018) stated that regular tobacco use can cause a range of cancers and smoking methamphetamine might fuel a severe form of dental decay known as "meth mouth."

**Injury:** This can occur during the administration of a drug, depending on the method. For example, injecting heroin with a needle can lead to skin and muscle damage at the point of injection, and many people take drugs by smoking, causing lung damage and respiratory illnesses.

Injury can also occur while intoxicated. Often, drug use impairs co-ordination and balance and can lead to falls and injuries. Driving while under the influence of alcohol and other drugs is criminal in most countries and caused 28 percent of all deaths related to traffic across the United States in 2016. Some substances induce violent reactions in people and increase the likelihood of risky or confrontational behaviours.

**Overdose:** Taking too much of one substance or mixing substances together can result in an overdose. While this can also occur with medications and pharmaceuticals, it is more likely to occur in a person who takes a substance to alter their mood or for recreational purposes.

An overdose can result in coma and death. More than 10,300 Canadians died as a result of an apparent opioid-related overdose between January 2016 and September 2018. The Public Health Agency of Canada says, "During the first nine months of 2018, 3,286 Canadians lost their lives to apparent opioid-related overdoses."

**Cardiovascular health:** Many substances lead to spikes in blood pressure and heart rate, placing strain on the heart and blood vessels and increasing the risk of stroke, heart attack, and death.

**Loss of hygiene and routine:** Addiction can become an all-encompassing feature in a person's life, and reward systems in the brain can rewire to prioritize the substance or behaviour at the root of the addiction over nutrition, resolving stressful situations, and hygiene.

Addiction can also mean that a person dedicates large sums of money each month to obtaining the substance, increasing the risk of poor nutrition. In some cases, addiction can lead to homelessness, greatly reducing protection and resources and increasing exposure to the elements.

**Fetal damage:** If a woman takes substances while pregnant, this can lead to congenital anomalies or even death in the fetus.

## Story Share by Alison
## Heroin Stole my Life

*In the beginning, addicts may have used heroin as an escape—an escape from worry, pain, fear, and ultimately, all of reality. It appears the drug "helped" them deal with things like stress and sadness by covering up the pain for a short time. But over time, the addiction consumes every thought in every corner of the person's mind, until eventually, that person can only be defined as a heroin addict, because he or she has no other concerns than finding his or her next 'fix.'*

"One night, I wanted to go to a party, but I had to get some [heroin] in my system first. So, after we both shot up, my friend and I hopped in the car and I started driving. Before I knew it, I had wrapped my car around a tree.

"For some reason, I was okay—at least as far as I could tell. Then I looked over, and I knew my friend was dead. He was also my cousin.

"I ended up doing jail time for involuntary manslaughter. If I had had it [heroin] on me at the time, I would have gotten life [in prison]. But I didn't.

"There's not a day that goes by that I don't think about [my cousin]. He was just the sweetest, most genuine person. To be honest, he was the only truly good person I had ever known in my life up to that point.

"From the day I started using, I never stopped. Within one week, I had gone from snorting heroin to shooting it. Within one month, I was addicted and going through all my money. I sold everything of value that I owned and eventually everything that my mother owned. Within one year, I had lost everything.

"I sold my car, lost my job, was kicked out of my mother's house, was $25,000 in credit card debt. I lied, I stole, and I cheated.

# CHAPTER 5: ADDICTION

*"I was raped, beaten, mugged, robbed, arrested, homeless, sick, and desperate. I knew that nobody could sustain a lifestyle like that very long, and I knew that death was imminent. If anything, death was better than a life as a junkie."*

## Story Share by Sunny
## The Truth about Life as a Heroin Addict

*"My skin was pale grey, my pupils perpetually dilated. I was jittery, my mannerisms were spastic, my dialogue was jumpy and curse laden. I was calling [my dealer] all the time. And finally, after a month, he told me I was too high maintenance and never to bother him again. I had been fired by my drug dealer."*

But because of the network of dealers she had become acquainted with, she had no problem finding more of the drug. At one point, she was using so much that she would have two to three dealers coming to her house daily, because one would sell her as much as they could, and then when she ran out, she'd just call the next in line.

Eventually, her paranoia got so bad that she stopped leaving her apartment and basically shut everyone out of her life—friends, family, everyone.

*"My body started to deteriorate. My skin bruised easily from lack of sleep, and I had deep circles under my eyes. My hands and feet swelled to the size of balloons. Once, I mistakenly applied pink nail polish under my eyes, thinking it was concealer…*

*"I'd stay awake for days at a time, sometimes for a full week. I never ate when I was using, and I drank only alcohol—water, juice, and pop made me sick. I guzzled olive oil for calories, and sometimes, to clear my clogged sinuses, I would drink Frank's Red-hot straight out of the bottle. It burned my mouth and eyes, but the shock would do the trick: I could stop blowing my nose and blow lines instead.*

*"By this time, I weighed 102 pounds. I kept thinking that I would spontaneously return to my previous self—when I was using less—when I felt validated and happy, when my life seemed exciting and glamorous…*

*"My paranoia descended into full-fledged psychosis. I suspected that everyone was on drugs—my neighbours, the concierge in my building, the barista at Starbucks. I saw men pointing machine guns at me from the shadows in the corner of my living room.*

"When I watched TV, I thought the shows were trying to tell me something: characters on a kids' cartoon would say 'Jump!' and I would jump; they would say 'Touch your nose,' and I'd touch my nose.

"One day, a dealer I was seeing told me to go out on the balcony of my condo … that a plane was coming to save me from this hell I was living. I gingerly made my way to the balcony and slid open the door, wanting to make him happy. I stepped into the cool night air and tried to climb over the railing. As I started my descent, he screamed, and rushed outside and grabbed me. He'd told me no such thing. I had hallucinated the conversation…"

## Story Share by Anonymous
## I Found Myself Taking More and More Pills to Keep Up

*I cannot tell you my name, or where I live, or even the specialty within which I practice medicine. I cannot do so for I have been shamed, embarrassed, and at times stigmatized. Even today, years later, I fear retribution, liability, and even prosecution. Some of this may have been deserved at one time, but today my story is one of success. It is a story of hope, of support, and of recovery. I share this intimate tale so that you, my colleagues and friends in the medical field, can hear the human side of addictive disease, of its treacherous grip, and of the freedom and confidence from which I have emerged from this terrifying illness.*

*My drug use did not begin until medical school. I was never a drinker in high school or even in college, nor did I use drugs socially. Then, one evening when I was finding it hard to stay awake to study for an organic chemistry exam, a friend directed me to some stimulants that were available in sample form. The result was perfect. I began using the pills, rather innocently, whenever I needed a boost. To me, it was like a cup of coffee, only better. I soon learned that I could order the pills on the internet and have a supply whenever it was needed*

*Upon graduation, I entered practice determined to be the best doctor possible. I spent a great deal of time with my patients, who kept coming back. My patient load grew exponentially, and I had trouble keeping pace. I had no experience running a business, was working long hours, and was unable to juggle the growing load. I found myself taking more and more pills just to keep up, and then*

## CHAPTER 5: ADDICTION

*even more pills to get me to sleep again. I gave little thought to this drug use. After all, I was no street junkie making covert deals in dark alleys. I was a good doctor, with many patients, using my medical knowledge to make the path toward success a bit smoother. So, I thought.*

*My drug use escalated. In addition to internet orders, I would write prescriptions in the names of my family members. Suddenly, my uncle had knee pain, my father-in-law back problems, my aunt arthritis. I did not think about the record I was establishing of their purported use, nor did I think about the records of my own prescribing practices. I was out of control, but getting by, taking many pills to get through each day.*

*Throughout this time, I still felt on top. Despite my drug use, I was a physician with a thriving practice. I provided quality care and had no patient complaints. I had a wife and children that relied upon me and saw me as a great provider. My friends and family admired me. I was respected in the community. I enjoyed my status and felt it was deserved, having achieved academically as well as socially since childhood.*

*And then one day, the Drug Enforcement Agency came to the door inquiring about fraudulent prescriptions. The reality of the situation took months to sink in. My reaction was disbelief. I was no druggie engaged in covert activities, and I was certainly no criminal. I was an admired and respected physician. I was sure the entire misunderstanding would be cleared up with a smile and an apology. I could not have been more wrong.*

*The shame and magnitude of my tumble was immeasurable. Not only did I face the legal and professional ramifications of having written improper prescriptions, but I had to cope with the personal humiliation of a fall from grace. I was no longer the icon of success I had worked a lifetime to achieve. I was now tainted, not only in the eyes of my colleagues but also, for the very first time, in my own.*

*Fortunately, when everything was crumbling around me, I got support and advice. With the guidance of Physician Health Services (PHS), I got into a treatment program that helped me realize that I suffered from a virulent illness and was both worthy and deserving of help. I was medically detoxified from the effects of the medications I had now stopped taking. I learned to take responsibility for my behaviours, but also to recognize that I had been sick and could certainly get well. I learned that addiction would be a lifelong condition, but not a lifelong impairment, and I agreed to a long-term monitoring contract with PHS. To comply with this contract, I had to work hard. I saw a therapist to address issues of addiction, shame, honesty, and interpersonal relationships. I submitted to regular and random drug screens. I attended support group meetings, met with sponsors and mentors, and in doing so, changed my life dramatically.*

*After months of treatment, out of state, learning about my disease and learning about myself, I came back home feeling strong. I was healthy, drug free, clear thinking, and ready to pull my career back together. Unfortunately, my career was not yet ready for me. Even though I had never had a malpractice case and had never harmed a patient, there would be months of waiting for the licensing board to address my petition to go back to work. I would be investigated, questioned, and challenged. This process lasted for months on end, and when I did get my license, it was with extensive restrictions and requirements for informing everyone with whom I had professional contact of my "probationary status" and of my disease. These required disclosures then led to a new round of inquiries by third-party credentialing agencies, without which I could not sustain a practice, so I began the journey again. More questions, more disclosures, more humiliation.*

*The greatest challenge of all was the subsequent public disgrace. The day my license was finally restored, a press release was issued informing the public of my professional discipline. My name became front-page news, highlighted by lurid references to drugs, diversion, and criminal activity. There was no mention of my recovery from illness nor of the months and years of personal work and growth I had achieved. What was to be a day of celebration had become a day of pain and shame. My daughter had a soccer game that day, and through tears, even she had to face the humiliation of what I had hoped was well in my past.*

*Although I was angry and frustrated with the obstacles I was facing, I now had the tools to deal with this stress. Through PHS, I had a physician support group where I could meet and learn from other doctors who faced these same struggles. I had an outlet for sharing my experiences and for learning from example that there was indeed hope for my future. And most importantly, I had my sobriety and my health.*

*Ultimately, I did return to practice. It was no easy journey. The process took years. During this time, I was doubted by others, and I doubted myself. But now I am stronger. I have the confidence of knowing that whatever ills befall me, I can heal. As a result, I am a better healer. My practice is now as successful as ever. I continue to be board certified in my specialty. I continue to provide quality care.*

## CHAPTER 5: ADDICTION

*I also have additional contributions to make to the profession. I am more open-mind and less likely to pass judgment. I have learned that medicine is not about being powerful or respected, but about being respectful and compassionate. I have learned that physicians, like all people, have the susceptibility to become ill and the capacity to become well. However, to encourage wellness, we (as a profession) need to provide resources and nurturance, not shame and humiliation. I am now sober and can't imagine facing life any other way. And I share this story so that all my colleagues in the medical field will know that they, too, can embark successfully upon this journey.*

### In case you need this today

---

You are not a failure;

You are not a waste of time;

You are loved;

You are wanted;

I believe in you;

You got this.

## Story Share by Anonymous
## A Mother's Bouts with Pain

*This story of heroin addiction might be a different one than you'd expect. She is a stay-at-home mother who became dependent on prescription pain medication. That is where her heroin story starts. Following the birth of her second child, she was prescribed Vicodin for pain. As the Vicodin ran out, her craving for it continued, and she needed more.*

*To get it, she would visit her doctor and fabricate a reason why she needed the painkiller. When it ran out, she'd create another reason why she needed more. The ruse worked and worked well. From one doctor alone, she was holding prescriptions that could be filled for hundreds of pills each month. And her doctor wasn't the only one being fooled. She carried out a normal, suburban lifestyle. Her daughter noted that she was a mom that "everybody looked up to and wanted to be." In contrast, she was self-medicating with up to twenty painkillers every day. The pills made her feel like a better version of herself. She believed the medication made her better in most every way. She lived this way for two years, until she was out of medication and got a dose of reality from the same doctor that was prescribing the meds. How it happened was by way of a loved one: her husband. Faced with a sobering reality, she reached out to her ex-husband. He in turn spoke with the doctor issuing the prescriptions, who responded by placing the blame on her; she should have been smart enough not to abuse the medication she was given. That was a turning point. She promised to stop, but it was far easier said than done.*

*The addiction continued. Her behaviour changed, however. Instead of solely relying on doctor prescriptions, she started finding her fix wherever she could. She would rummage through her friends' and families' medicine cabinets looking for more. She would telephone refill requests in on prescriptions and say she was merely picking them up for someone else. Eventually her run ran out. A pharmacy called the issuing doctor of a prescription only to confirm that the refill was not authorized. She avoided prosecution but did have a run in with the law. The result was her agreeing to in-patient residential rehab.*

*Although her time in rehab was coined a success, her struggles with addiction continued. A decade after her becoming addicted to opioids, she moved out of her home, leaving her husband and two children behind. Her addiction progressed.*

# CHAPTER 5: ADDICTION

*Moving from prescription to street drugs, she dabbled in crystal meth and then back to opiates in the form of heroin. It wasn't long until she was living in a drug house with over a dozen other addicts. Living conditions were poor. The home served one purpose to its residents: getting their fix. Her downward spiral had landed in a dangerous place of full-blown addiction.*

*The suburban mother of two reflects on that time: "I lost it all. And it really didn't matter to me. If I could get high, it was okay."*

*To pay for heroin, she began selling and selling in high volume. It wasn't going unnoticed by the local narcotics authorities. And when she sold drugs to a narcotics officer, her most serious legal wrangling began. To avoid jail time, she opted into a methadone program and attended programs to help keep her off heroin, opioids, and any other drug. She still struggles with addiction today, but is lucky to be alive. Her path often ends with a much more tragic event.*

# CHAPTER 6

## ANXIETY

Even though occasional anxiety may be temporary, it sometimes persists after the event causing it is over. A prolonged feeling of fear and unease can signify an anxiety disorder. People with anxiety disorders experience worse anxiety experiences, which persist over a long period of time. When it comes to this level, intervention is required to get the person to normal mental health. Some of the common types of anxiety disorders include post-traumatic stress disorder (PTSD), social disorder, panic disorder, and specific phobias (Beck, Emery & Greenberg, 2005). Researchers are yet to establish the main causes of anxiety disorders. However, there is an argument that such disorders are as a result of a combination of many things that take place over a period. Such events change the brain, leading to the mental disorders.

People with anxiety shows symptoms such as panic, restlessness, sleep problems, dry mouth, shortness of breath, nausea, dizziness, and tense muscles. Once diagnosed, an individual can be treated to resume a normal life just like other people. In most cases, treatments are psychological as well as aiming at managing the symptoms. Medication includes use of antidepressants and other types of medications (Hoge, Ivkovic & Fricchione, 2012). Psychotherapy includes counselling the affected person. Cognitive behavioural therapy is the most common therapy done on anxiety patients, as well as managing the symptoms through things like healthy eating and proper sleep, which help a lot.

## Types of Anxiety Disorders

There are various types of anxiety disorders, which include post-traumatic stress disorder, panic disorders, as well as general anxiety disorders. PTSD is associated with traumatic events experienced in life. Some of these traumatic events may include loss of a close friend, accident scenes, and many more. These events affect an individual psychologically and can lead to anxiety if not taken care of (Beck, Emery & Greenberg, 2005). PTSD is associated with flashbacks or night sweats. When such happens, a person develops fear of experiencing the traumatic events that initially led to the disorder. Panic disorder is associated with frequent panic and fear without a clear cause. The most common type of anxiety is the generalized anxiety disorder. This happens when an individual worries about life issues every day. General anxiety may differ from one person to the other.

## Causes and Risk Factors of Anxiety Disorders

Research is yet to conclude what causes anxiety disorders. However, most of them have been linked with various factors. These factors explain why some people are at a higher risk of developing anxiety disorders than other people. Some of the possible causes of these include biological factors and environmental stressors. Some people are born with temperamental traits of shyness. Others face behavioural inhibition in childhood, which affects the person later in adulthood (Beck, Emery & Greenberg, 2005). Exposure to environmental stressors has also been known to cause anxiety disorders. This can either happen in childhood or adulthood. Research has also established that anxiety runs in some families, hence having those genes is the reason some people have anxiety while others fail to have such disorders even after being exposed to the same events.

Some physical health conditions are responsible for anxiety disorders as well, such conditions include heart arrhythmias or thyroid problems (Beck, Emery & Greenberg, 2005). Substances such as caffeine and medications can also produce anxiety signs. This explains why physical examination is crucial when it comes to diagnosis of anxiety disorders.

### Living in Hell

———

Depression is when you don't care about anything.

Anxiety is when you care too much about everything.

And having both is like living in hell (whatever that is).

## Signs and Symptoms of Anxiety

Anxiety manifests itself in different signs and symptoms. Even though most of these symptoms are similar for many of people having anxiety, they can differ from one person to the next. One of the main symptoms of anxiety is panic or a feeling of fear. This is common to almost every person having this disorder. People tend to have increased fear of the unknown. Panic is a result of fear of the unknown. Sleeping problems are also common with people with anxiety. Since they worry much about their lives and the unknown, they find it difficult to sleep comfortably. They tend to wake up from sleep from time to time and experience irregular sleep patterns. It's not strange to find an individual spending a whole night awake (Beck, Emery & Greenberg, 2005). When this happens, it's most likely that the person is dealing with an anxiety disorder.

Lack of concentration is also a sign of anxiety disorder. This is as a result of excessive worry about encountering the feared experience. Due to the fear for the unknown, people tend to worry too much and end up failing to concentrate even on important issues. An individual's mind is always divided between the reality and what may happen in the future. People try as much as possible not to encounter this feared experience or event. Excessive worrying does not allow an individual to stay calm, even when the situation demands it (Beck, Emery & Greenberg, 2005). Fear also leads to excessive sweating and sometimes coldness. This is as a result of heightened fear of the traumatizing experience. Shortness of breath is also associated with anxiety disorders. This is caused by excessive fear and panic.

Heart palpitations are also associated with anxiety in most people. Although it may signify another health problem, it is linked with anxiety when detected together with other anxiety signs and symptoms. Heart palpitations alone cannot be enough to signify that an individual is having anxiety disorder. Other signs of this mental disorder include dry mouth, nausea, dizziness, and tense muscles (Beck, Emery & Greenberg, 2005). In most cases, these symptoms are common for most of the anxiety types. However, some of them are unique to some of the types of anxiety disorders, such as phobias. In addition, these symptoms continue manifesting themselves up to the time when the person goes through the necessary treatment to deal with the problem. When not solved, the symptoms can remain with the person for as long as the person lives. The kind of support an individual gets when going through these situations determines the extent of the anxiety symptoms to be manifested. When people are without the necessary social support, they tend to have heightened anxiety levels.

## Diagnosing Anxiety Disorder

Anxiety disorder can be difficult to diagnose, since it involves some confusing signs and symptoms. First, it starts with symptoms that are examined by a medical doctor or a psychiatrist. A conversation with a doctor or a psychologist can help them establish if a person is having anxiety disorder or not (Hoge, Ivkovic & Fricchione, 2012). This is from the symptoms as explained by the patient. When the doctor discovers anxiety symptoms in a patient, the doctor can ask about the medical history of the person. This is because anxiety disorder is known to run in families. Medical history of the person can tell if the person is from a family known to have anxiety disorders. If the person is from such a family, it's most likely that the person is having an anxiety disorder.

The next step is to run medical tests on the person. This is to rule out other illnesses as the cause of the symptoms shown by the patient. For instance, an individual may have heart complications, which may be caused by either anxiety disorder or other illnesses. Medical tests will show whether the symptoms are caused by heart illnesses (Hoge, Ivkovic & Fricchione, 2012). When such illnesses are ruled out, it remains that anxiety is the most likely cause of the symptoms. This is because there are no medical tests that can diagnose anxiety. After medical doctors are done with the tests, and it's proven that anxiety is the most likely cause of the symptoms, the next option is to send the person to a psychiatrist. Other mental-health specialists can also be of help in such cases (Hoge, Ivkovic & Fricchione, 2012). Diagnosis also reveals the intensity of the symptoms in order to determine the next course of action. When the symptoms are intense, it shows that the person in dire need of treatment. In such cases, the symptoms prevent the person from carrying out normal activities in life.

## Treating Anxiety

Anxiety disorder can be treated with the necessary measures in place. This may involve either medical treatment or psychological treatment and sometimes both. In most cases, mental disorders are treated using psychological means. Treatment seeks to help the person live a normal life. Medical treatment involves the use of medications such as antidepressants. In most cases, anxiety disorders are associated with depression. To deal with these, antidepressants are prescribed for anxiety patients (Hoge, Ivkovic & Fricchione, 2012). Antidepressants include fluoxetine and escitalopram. When taken, they help reduce anxiety symptoms in the short run. In addition, anticonvulsant medications are used to treat anxiety disorders. These are mostly taken for epilepsy. To make treatments work better, antipsychotic medications are taken by those going through anxiety treatment. They also help lower the levels of anxiety in an individual. Some of these medications are clonazepam and alprazolam. These are mostly prescribed for patients suffering general anxiety disorders.

Mental disorders are mostly treated using psychological means. These may involve counseling the patients. Psychotherapy is mostly used in psychological intervention for anxiety disorders. This is a type of counselling to help patients deal with their mental response to anxiety. Psychiatrists talk to the patient about their response to anxiety. Such interventions help the patient perfectly deal with anxiety disorders. Psychiatrists educate the patients on how to respond to anxiety and help restore the patient's mental health (Craske, 1999).

Psychiatrists are important when it comes to helping these patients go through the healing process. They walk with the patients throughout the journey to ensure that they overcome the anxiety burden. Cognitive behavioural therapy is the other psychological intervention used to treat anxiety disorder. This is a psychotherapy intervention that teaches anxiety patients how to recognize and change behaviours and thoughts leading to anxiety. Solving the problem starts right from recognizing the causes of the disorder. Patients are taught how to identify these causes at an early stage and then overcome them. Thought patterns leading to anxiety disorder can be recognized and prevented before they lead to anxiety. Since it is difficult to discover these patterns, patients are taught how to discover them and overcome them before they lead to anxiety disorder (Craske, 1999).

Anxiety patients need attention and care from other people. They need social support to overcome this disorder. This is where family members and close friends must play a role in dealing with anxiety disorder, to provide social support to anxiety patients and help them overcome the problem whilst having loving conversations. This a role that must be played by those close to the person. Family members and friends are also needed to help a patient go through the healing process. Healing is a journey that needs social support to complete, since anxiety victims are already mentally weakened, outside parties are needed to help them overcome the challenges brought on by the disorder.

## Managing Anxiety Disorder Symptoms

Unlike treatment, managing anxiety symptoms helps patients live a normal life and can even lead to slow healing over a period. With the following steps, an individual can reduce the intensity of the symptoms. Some of the steps towards managing anxiety disorders include cutting down some foods and drinks known to heighten the symptoms. Some of these drinks include caffeine-rich drinks such as tea, coffee, chocolate, energy drinks, and cola. Caffeine is known to alter the mood of an individual when taken (Hoge, Ivkovic & Fricchione, 2012). This can make anxiety symptoms get worse, since mood is at the centre of these symptoms. Avoiding them ensures that an individual experiences a stable mood, which translates to fewer anxiety symptoms.

Managing eating patterns also helps manage the symptoms of anxiety on people. Exercising is wholeheartedly recommended, as well as getting enough sleep. Exercise such as jogging helps in releasing chemicals in the brain, cutting down stress. It also improves an individual's mood. Sleep issues are common with anxiety patients. As a result, anxiety patients are advised to get enough sleep (Hoge, Ivkovic & Fricchione, 2012). Getting adequate rest is important to reduce anxiety symptoms. People having anxiety disorder are advised to have a sleeping routine and follow it perfectly. Lastly, people having anxiety disorder are also advised to consult their doctors before they take any step. Some medicines have chemicals that can worsen the symptoms. Doctors can realize such medications and advise the patients against them.

Anxiety is a common mental disorder that can be difficult to diagnose in people. People can live with anxiety without being been noticed or the disorder affecting their normal lives. However, when the disorder becomes worse, and symptoms manifest, an individual is required to seek medical intervention. Since the disorder is a mental one, psychological intervention is the most effective. Medication are only used to reduce the intensity of the symptoms and help the patients go through the healing process (Beck, Emery & Greenberg, 2005).

After experiencing some of the symptoms, such as panic, fear, dizziness, shortness of breath, and many more, they are advised to seek intervention. Not everyone will have the disorder after going through the same experiences. Biological factors make some people more prone to anxiety disorder than others. To help such patients live a normal live, psychiatrists are required to take them through a process of healing. Social support is also needed from family members and friends.

## Story Share by Author
## "I'm here NATO"

*As most TAVs (technical assistance visit) start, we were briefed on our mission. Tuzla was the destination this time, as it falls into our AOR (Area of Responsibility), which was a US Air Force Base for the Sikorsky UH-60 Blackhawks. Tuzla was approximately 120 kilometres from Sarajevo north through all the switchbacks some over 180 degrees—yes, 180—going back where you came from. If you're not aware of Sarajevo and its communities, it is surrounded by mountains, with Sarajevo being the bowl in the middle. The trip to Tuzla is approximately four hours in convoy from the city. On our trip, we passed through a small town called Olovo. As we were leaving the outskirts of the town, I heard four pops right behind my window (backseat). I said, "What the hell was that?" The crew shrugged their shoulders, as they didn't know either.*

## CHAPTER 6: ANXIETY

*On arrival to Tuzla, we needed to check in, as protocol dictates, and I noticed four bullet holes in a four-inch grouping right behind my head. When I thought back to our route and going through Olovo, I realized that the four pops I heard was local sniper fire. I felt sick to my stomach trying not to vomit, swallowing extremely hard, knowing that if that sniper wanted me dead, I would be. I reflect on this now, thinking they were warning shots saying, "I'm here NATO."*

**Story Share Anonymous**
**When I realized I was struggling with Anxiety**

*I've been suffering from anxiety, panic attacks, and depression pretty much my whole life. I can remember so plainly the first day I had an attack. I was nineteen years old, at a friend's having coffee, and all of a sudden my heart was palpating and my hands were shaky and my vision was blurred a bit. I had no idea what was going on, so I excused myself, went home, told my boyfriend, and we made a doctor's appointment. Upon seeing the doctor, he explained, "Oh, you're just having an anxiety attack. Take these Ativan when you feel one coming on!"*

*Of course, I figured they would go away, and the pills were useless to me. The next step was to see a counselor, who also tried to push pills. I didn't want that. For the next year, I felt very alone and scared, and felt like I was going crazy—lack of sleep, overeating, and avoiding people like the plague. I knew I had to figure this out and figure it out fast, so I could lead somewhat of a normal life again. So I started analyzing everything in my life and tried to figure out what could be causing me to feel this way. After a lot of thinking and contemplating, I started focusing on my relationship with my boyfriend at that time. You see, he was a great guy, but not the one for me. He wasn't allowing me to be me. I wanted so much more, and more happiness and love in my life, but I was feeling sorry for him and stayed in the relationship for six years.*

*I realized that the people, at that time, in my life were so negative and weren't really true friends to me. I felt like there was no one to talk to. I remember a lot of the ways I got through things was through alcohol, so I was numb. (Stupid, right?)*

*Until one day I had enough, and said, "Girl, either you can stay a hermit and dwell on this crap or get up and start living your life. Stop caring so much about what other people think and push yourself daily." Baby steps at first, of course.*

*I did. I inched my way back out into the world, little by little, through a lot of positive self-talk, and met the man, amongst all this chaos, whom I've now been with over twenty-two years. He helped me through so much of my fear by always saying, "You can do it. I know you can." I got my GED, which I never thought I'd be able to do, and a lot of other accomplishments. Now don't get me wrong, I still struggle with things day to day, but I think back and say, "No way will I let you win again. I'm better than that."*

*I still have a long way to go, but I'm so happy I can share my story with others. I could go on and on and blame this on a lot of things, like my upbringing, which was by no means great, but you know ... I'm not sure why it happened. I just live my life day to day and try to keep a positive attitude in life and be happy.*

## Story Share by Melisa
## My Heart was About to Explode

*I have always been an anxious person since childhood, worrying about things rather than playing with other kids my age, but my problems really started around thirteen years ago. After losing my best friend to suicide, and my partner at the time leaving me, weeks after having our daughter, I thought I was coping really well. Then one day, I was in town with a friend, and we were standing in a queue at the bank and were chatting away, and suddenly everything went hazy. The only way I can describe it is that everything seemed distant, and I could see people and see their mouths moving, but I couldn't seem to understand what they were saying. I can remember my friend shaking me and asking if I was okay, and feeling like my heart was about to explode out of my chest, and needing to find the nearest chair as my legs felt as though they couldn't hold me up.*

*I felt like something was wrong and would go as far as to say I felt I was dying, and I just needed to get home. We left the city in a hurry, with my friend crying with fear, because she didn't know what was happening to me. That was my biggest mistake, as the only place I felt safe then was home, and it became my prison for seven years. I was forced by my family to seek medical help, and my family made me feel I was overreacting. Asking for help every time I needed shopping was degrading, and I felt I was constantly putting my friends and family out. The worst day of my life came when my daughter fell and broke her wrist,*

# CHAPTER 6: ANXIETY

*and she was terrified and crying, and I had to watch her being taken to hospital by someone else as the panic had a too big a hold on me.*

*My children used to go and spend weekends with their father, and during this time, I also developed monophobia (fear of being left alone), and as soon as they left the house, I would have panic attack after panic attack. There is also nothing like the feeling of watching friends and family go on holiday and knowing I couldn't take my children anywhere. My eldest son couldn't stand to see me suffering and moved out at seventeen to live with his girlfriend, but my other child was my life saver. She looked after me in a way I can never repay. She never once asked anything of me, and we spent many hours having great times together at home, playing games and watching movies. She was the reason I was determined to recover.*

*First step, doctors. Endless counselling… Going over my past, didn't help at all. CBT helped for six sessions, but then it stopped and was made to feel a failure for it not working. I spent hours and hours of time browsing the internet and trying fake panic attack remedies, and was about to give up when a link for No Panic came up on google. Thank God I clicked on it, as I nearly didn't and would never have been where I am today.*

# CHAPTER 7

## DEMENTIA

Dementia is not a specific disease. It's an overall term that describes a group of symptoms associated with a decline in memory or other thinking skills severe enough to reduce a person's ability to perform everyday activities. Alzheimer's disease accounts for 60 to 80 percent of cases. Vascular dementia, which occurs after a stroke, is the second-most common dementia type. But there are many other conditions that can cause symptoms of dementia, including some that are reversible, such as thyroid problems and vitamin deficiencies.

Dementia is often incorrectly referred to as "senility" or "senile dementia," which reflects the formerly widespread but incorrect belief that serious mental decline is a normal part of aging.

## Memory Loss and Symptoms of Dementia

While symptoms of dementia can vary greatly, at least two of the following core mental functions must be significantly impaired to be considered dementia:

- Memory
- Communication and language
- Ability to focus and pay attention
- Reasoning and judgment
- Visual perception

People with dementia may have problems with short-term memory, keeping track of a purse or wallet, paying bills, planning and preparing meals, remembering appointments, or traveling out of the neighbourhood.

Many dementias are progressive, meaning symptoms start out slowly and gradually get worse. If you or someone you know is experiencing memory difficulties or other changes in thinking skills, don't ignore them. See a doctor soon to determine the cause. Professional evaluation may detect a treatable condition. And even if symptoms suggest dementia, early diagnosis allows a person to get the maximum benefit from available treatments and provides an opportunity to volunteer for clinical trials or studies. It also provides time to plan.

## Causes of Dementia

Dementia is caused by damage to brain cells. This damage interferes with the ability of brain cells to communicate with each other. When brain cells cannot communicate normally, thinking, behaviour, and feelings can be affected.

The brain has many distinct regions, each of which is responsible for different functions (for example, memory, judgment, and movement). When cells in a region are damaged, that region cannot carry out its functions normally.

Different types of dementia are associated with types of brain-cell-damaged regions of the brain. For example, in Alzheimer's disease, high levels of certain proteins inside and outside brain cells make it hard for brain cells to stay healthy and communicate with each other. The brain region called the hippocampus is the centre of learning and memory in the brain, and the brain cells in this region are often the first to be damaged. That's why memory loss is often one of the earliest symptoms of Alzheimer's.

While most changes in the brain that cause dementia are permanent and worsen over time, thinking and memory problems caused by the following conditions may improve when the condition is treated or addressed:

- Depression
- Medication side effects
- Excess use of alcohol
- Thyroid problems
- Vitamin deficiencies

## Diagnosis of Dementia

There is no one test to determine if someone has dementia. Doctors diagnose Alzheimer's and other types of dementia based on a careful medical history, a physical examination, laboratory tests, and the characteristic changes in thinking, day-to-day function, and behaviour associated with each type. Doctors can determine that a person has dementia with a high level of certainty. But it's harder to determine the exact type of dementia, because the symptoms and brain changes of different dementias can overlap. In some cases, a doctor may diagnose "dementia" and not specify a type. If this occurs, it may be necessary to see a specialist such as a neurologist or neuropsychologist.

## Dementia Risk and Prevention

Some risk factors for dementia, such as age and genetics, cannot be changed. But researchers continue to explore the impact of other risk factors on brain health and prevention of dementia. Some of the most active areas of research in risk reduction and prevention include cardiovascular factors, physical fitness, and diet.

- Cardiovascular risk factors: Your brain is nourished by one of your body's richest networks of blood vessels. Anything that damages blood vessels anywhere in your body can damage blood vessels in your brain, depriving brain cells of vital food and oxygen. Blood vessel changes in the brain are linked to vascular dementia. They often are present along with changes caused by other types of dementia, including Alzheimer's disease and dementia with Lewy bodies. These changes may interact to cause faster decline or make impairments more severe. You can help protect your brain with some of the same strategies that protect your heart: Don't smoke; take steps to keep your blood pressure, cholesterol, and blood sugar within recommended limits; and maintain a healthy weight.

- Physical exercise: Regular physical exercise may help lower the risk of some types of dementia. Evidence suggests exercise may directly benefit brain cells by increasing blood and oxygen flow to the brain.

- Diet: What you eat may have its greatest impact on brain health through its effect on heart health. The best current evidence suggests that heart-healthy eating patterns, such as the Mediterranean diet, also may help protect the brain. A Mediterranean diet includes relatively little red meat and emphasizes whole grains, fruits, and vegetables, fish and shellfish, and nuts, olive oil, and other healthy fats.

Alzheimer's disease and other common forms of dementia, including vascular dementia, dementia with Lewy bodies, and front temporal dementia, are progressive conditions, with symptoms worsening over time as the disease progresses. Learn more about the stages of dementia and what to expect from your loved one as dementia progresses. (Sauer, 2018)

Although the two terms are often used interchangeably, Alzheimer's disease and dementia are two different terms. Dementia is an umbrella term used to describe several conditions, and it includes Alzheimer's as well as other conditions with shared symptoms. More than mere forgetfulness, an individual must have trouble with at least two of the following areas to be diagnosed with dementia.

- Memory
- Communication and Speech
- Focus and Concentration
- Reasoning Judgment
- Visual Perception

# Different Categories of Dementia

- No Dementia (category A-C)
- Initial (category D)
- Intermediate (category E-F)

- Final (category G)

## Category A–C Dementia (No Dementia)

### Category A

In Phase1 of dementia, there are no signs of dementia. The person functions normally, and is mentally healthy. People with no dementia diagnosis are considered Category A. There are no signs or symptoms, no memory loss, behavioural problems, or anything else associated with the onset of dementia.

### Category B

From there, the disease progresses into phase 2, also known as very mild cognitive decline. In this stage, there is normal forgetfulness that are often attributed to aging. In this stage, caregivers may start to notice some level of forgetfulness, but symptoms of dementia are still not apparent to medical professionals or loved ones. In this early stage, caregiving is about finding a balance between independence and assistance.

### Category C

The last stage in this category is Category C, mild cognitive decline. At this stage, loved ones may notice signs of cognitive decline as their loved one experiences increased forgetfulness, decreased performance at work, speech difficulty, and difficulty focusing on everyday tasks. This stage is also known as mild cognitive impairment (MCI) and it crucial that caregivers recognize the signs of this stage for early diagnosis and intervention. When in doubt, assume your loved one can accomplish a given task on his or her own, unless there is an immediate risk to safety.

### Category D (Initial Phase Dementia)

Early-phase dementia has only one category: Category D, moderate cognitive decline. This phase lasts an average of two years and cognitive issues can be detected during a medical interview and exam. People in this category will have difficulty concentrating, will forget recent events, and will have difficulty managing finances and traveling alone to new locations. Additionally, they may have trouble socializing and begin withdrawing from friends and family. In this category, caregivers should make a concerted effort to actively engage the person with dementia. Caregivers will have a more involved role in this stage and subsequent stages. Caregivers should create a daily care plan and make adjustments to schedules as needed to provide the necessary level of care, while also seeking physical and emotional support from other caregivers.

- Misplacing items
- Forgetting recent conversations or events
- Struggling to find the right words in a conversation
- Losing track of the day, date, or time
- Loss of interest in other people or activities
- Unwilling to try new things
- Increased feelings of anxiety, irritability, or depression
- Trouble remembering names when meeting new people
- Increased trouble planning or organizing

## Category E-F Dementia (Intermediate Phase Dementia)

### Category E

Lasting an average of four years, a person in mid-phase dementia now needs assistance to complete activities of daily living. In this category, signs and symptoms of dementia will be very easy to identify. Short-term memory will be mostly lost, and confusion and forgetfulness will be more pronounced throughout activities of daily living.

### Category F

In Category F of dementia, a person may start forgetting the names of close loved ones and have little memory of recent events. Communication is severely disabled, and delusions, compulsions, anxiety, and agitation may occur.

Symptoms of mid-phase dementia

- Problems sleeping and confusing day and night
- Behaving inappropriately in social settings
- Wandering or becoming lost
- Difficulty with perception
- Delusions and/or hallucinations
- Increased aggression and irritability
- Inability to recall personal history, address, and phone number
- Changes in sleep patterns may begin

## Category G (Final Phase Dementia)

This final category of dementia includes one stage: Category G, very severe cognitive decline, lasts an average of 2.5 years. A person in this category usually has no ability to speak or communicate and requires assistance with most activities, including walking. During this category, caregivers will focus mostly on providing comfort and quality of life. Care options may exceed what you feel you can provide at home, since around-the-clock care will be needed.

**Symptoms of Late-Phase Dementia**
- Difficulty eating and swallowing
- Considerable changes in weight (both loss and gain)
- Incontinence
- Gradual loss of speech
- Restlessness
- Angry outbursts due to confusion
- Increasingly vulnerable to infections, especially pneumonia

While the exact symptoms displayed in each category can differ from person to person, this information can be used as a guide, helping families know what to expect and when to expect it.

## Story Share by Anonymous
## Dementia is More than Memory

*"Dementia is more than memory. My brain and body are so tired that I can hardly cook my dinner." But she can't sleep in: "Something strange has been happening to me over the last four or five months. I'm waking up so early in the morning.*

*"My abilities to be able to cook are steadily diminishing… I am losing my ability to sequence, plan, prepare, and cook. I hate packing. I pick up one thing, put it down, look for another thing, look for the first thing you put down, and it's not there. You end up not knowing where anything is. You try to be logical, but you cannot be logical when you've got Alzheimer's.*

*"They talk about the losses you get with dementia, and yes, there have been many losses, but not so with my hearing. My hearing has been heightened, almost painfully. I can be out having a meal and the noise gets louder. It's just like a crescendo; it's terrible. I can't stand it, and I just want to finish the meal and get away.*

*"I seem to live in a state of constant anxiety, of not being able to cope with crossing the road, going shopping, having a shower. The day-to-day things have been more and more stressful and causing me panics. What does it feel like when I know that the slow progression is creeping in and getting more and more frequent? Frightening. Scary. I doubt myself."*

## Story Share by Carol
## How my Mum Slipped Away

*It was a cold rainy night when there was a knock my door. "Mum, what are you doing here?" I said to a freezing, soaking wet Mum. I took her in and gave her a towel and a hot drink. She finally explained she had lost her keys. Her speech had recently gone bad, but she always assured me it was because she had her teeth out.*

*I took her back to her house to see the front door wide open. I told Mum that was dangerous, and she shouldn't leave her door open. The keys were under her pillow. We laughed and that was that.*

*Another night, my telephone was ringing at three a.m., I hurried to answer it, and it was Mum asking, "Was I in?" I told her it was in the middle of the night, and she had to go back to bed. Again, we laughed, as often people get mixed up, don't they?*

*My sister Susan and I took Mum to the hospital. The doctor said that he thought it was Alzheimer's disease by her speech. I took Mum back to her house and went into the kitchen to make a coffee. 'What is Alzheimer's?' I thought, as I cried to myself. Mum came into the kitchen, switched the gas on, and walked away without lighting it. I switched the gas off and went into the living room, asking what she was doing. She explained that she was trying to light the fire in the living room. "What has that got to do with the cooker?" I yelled. What was going on?*

*Eventually Mum had a brain scan and the results came back: vascular dementia. She had had lots of TIA's (mini strokes) and each stroke had attacked different parts of her brain. Mum was very scared, and I remember telling her that we would make a promise to each other. My promise was to be with her till her last breath, and hers was that no matter what she forgot, she wouldn't forget we loved each other.*

*I was always close to Mum. We lived close by each other, and I became her sole caregiver. Eventually, I was told that she needed to go into a home. She went and hated it. Day after day, she would cry and beg me to take her home. My heart was being ripped out, so one morning, after her being there for five weeks, I walked into the home and I said, "Mum, do you want to come and live with me?" I will always remember the smile she gave me as she said, "Yes." It was lovely that first night at my house, with Mum and me and my three kids. Mum was so happy, and so was I. We were together.*

*As time went on, I became very protective towards her, and I spoke for her a lot if she was struggling. I would finish her sentences, but one day, she couldn't speak. A word would come out, but not the right word. I now urge everyone not to speak for the person. Let them speak, and so what if it's wrong? It doesn't matter.*

*I got Mum into a day centre, and the night before she first went, I got scared in case someone touched her in the wrong way. Before she went to bed, I showed her where no one could touch her. I went to bed broken at what I had just had to*

## CHAPTER 7: DEMENTIA

do. This was my mum who I was telling where her private places are. It was total a role reversal; suddenly I was Mum to my mum.

One day whilst I was colouring my hair, Mum came downstairs and asked me if I wanted a fight. She was angry, and I was scared. I said, "No, I don't want to fight with you." With that, she ran out of my house. I ran to the door crying, shouting at her to come back, but she carried on running. I couldn't run out in my pyjamas, with colour on my hair, so I grabbed the phone and rang the police. Everyone was looking for her. I couldn't stop being sick, because they couldn't find her.

Then at 4.30 p.m., the day centre bus brought her home. Apparently, they had picked her up on the road and never thought to tell me. I went berserk. Mum was oblivious to what had happened, but social services sectioned her. I was heartbroken. Mum was too. I had a caregiver breakdown. I felt such a complete failure. A bad daughter, and at the same time, a bad mum, as I'd shown my kids a side to their nan they never should have seen.

We had a fabulous six years with lots of fun, but Mum's needs changed, and I couldn't cope anymore. I visited every day and Mum would cry to come home; I was dying inside. But Mum did settle, and life got better, because I knew she was okay. She reached a point where she couldn't feed herself and kept falling over. They gave her meds to sit her down. Her speech went completely, and she aged to looking very old. She lost weight and looked so frail. That's how she was for about the next five years, in bed with padding around her.

On December 8, 2013, I got a phone call. Mum was in A&E with a suspected broken shoulder. Her heart was only sixty-nine, so it was strong, and she wasn't giving in. She lasted nineteen days, fifteen without food, and no meds, just pain relief to keep her comfortable. Boxing Day came and Mum peacefully grew her wings and flew to Heaven. I will always believe we both kept our promises. She knew I was there. She would always kick her little legs when she heard my voice. Eye contact was rare, but it was so nice when we did, as I could see my gorgeous Mum still there.

I will be honest; I thought I was going to die after Mum passed away. I was in a whirl, left with nothing. That's okay now, as I know she is dementia free as an angel. My angel. I got strong and became an ambassador for dementia with the Purple Angel Campaign. I spread awareness of dementia around Warrington. I want to help people living with dementia to live at home a lot longer, knowing people in shops won't rush or ridicule and will help them.

# CHAPTER 8

## SLEEP PROBLEMS

Most people have a TV in their room, or watch Netflix right before bed, or are scrolling social media right before bed. The issue with this is that most of the time the content you are consuming is negative and puts you in a bad state before bed. Make a point to turn off all electronics one to two hours before bed every night, and spend the last hour reading a good book or having a nice conversation with a loved one.

Never watch TV or go on your phone in bed. The blue light in electronic screens trick your brain into thinking it's still daytime, so your body won't produce the right amount of melatonin (the hormone that makes you sleepy) to help you sleep. Blue light wreaks havoc on your sleep. Don't do it. Set an alarm to go off at the same time every night, so you remember to turn off all electronics. Sleep disorders are changes in the way that you sleep.

A sleep disorder can affect your overall health, safety, and quality of life. Sleep deprivation can affect your ability to drive safely and increase your risk of other health problems. Some of the signs and symptoms of sleep disorders include excessive daytime sleepiness, irregular breathing or increased movement during sleep, and difficulty falling asleep.

There are many different types of sleep disorders. They're often grouped into categories that explain why they happen or how they affect you. Sleep disorders can also be grouped according to behaviours, problems with your natural sleep-wake cycles, breathing problems, difficulty sleeping, or how sleepy you feel during the day. (Mayo Clinic, 2019)

## Insomnia

Insomnia is when you have difficulty falling asleep or staying asleep throughout the night. Insomnia is a symptom that may result from stress, anxiety, depression, a serious medical condition, pain, or a substance-abuse issue. To help you overcome sleeplessness, you need to determine what type of insomnia is affecting you.

## *General Insomnia*

The catch-all term for sleeplessness is general insomnia, a classification of sleep disorders involving anyone who has difficulty getting to sleep at night (though it may also include people who wake up in the middle of the night or wake up too early). Overall, insomnia is simply defined as an overall insufficient amount and/or quality of sleep.

If you're only struggling to sleep occasionally, chances are your doctor will diagnose you with general insomnia. However, if your sleeplessness is the result of something more specific, your treatment may require a different approach.

Adults are not the only people to suffer with insomnia. Kids can also have significant sleep issues that can affect their ability to concentrate at school. Childhood insomnia is a serious issue that can negatively impact the natural development of a child.

Typically, doctors are reluctant to treat childhood insomnia with medication. The preferred approach is to have a conversation with the child to see what might be causing the problem. Often, it's related to stress or an irregular bedtime schedule.

## *Idiopathic Insomnia*

Idiopathic insomnia is one of the most serious sleep disorders. It's a lifelong problem that starts during a child's early years and lasts all the way into adulthood. Typically, idiopathic insomnia has nothing to do with stress, medication, or pain.

Idiopathic insomnia is the result of physical imbalance in the body. For example, it may be the result of an overactive awakening system or under active sleep trigger. What is clear is that those dealing with idiopathic insomnia need special treatment unique to their specific condition.

## *Insomnia Due to Substance Abuse*

There are several substances that can negatively affect the ability to sleep, including medication, caffeine, alcohol, and certain foods. Some medications can prevent sleep (which means you may need to take that medication earlier in the day). Caffeine can prevent the mind from effectively shutting down.

While alcohol can help one get to sleep, it may cause mid-night waking, and some foods (such as spicy foods) can cause indigestion and prevent the onset of sleep. Your challenge is to determine how you can remove the problem substance from your diet in order to resume sleeping effectively. This change may require the support of medical professionals.

## *Paradoxical Insomnia*

Paradoxical insomnia is a complicated matter that takes place without any clear evidence that sleeplessness is a problem. Those dealing with it may over-report the problem. That means they claim to have slept far less than they have.

There may be several explanations for paradoxical insomnia, but at its core, the issue is a mental-health matter. If someone you know appears to be dealing with this type of insomnia, encourage them to be open and honest with their physician about the issue. (Roberts, 2019)

## *Psychophysiological Insomnia*

It may sound highly complicated, but psychophysiological insomnia is both common and simple. It's essentially insomnia caused by excessive worrying about not being able to sleep. In effect, it's a vicious cycle: One does not sleep, so they worry about not sleeping, and for that reason, fail to get a good night's rest.

In many cases, people with this form of insomnia focus too much on being tired the next day as a result of not getting a full night's rest. In order to overcome these issues, they may need to be treated for anxiety or depression and take part in cognitive behavioural therapy.

CHAPTER 8: SLEEP PROBLEMS

# Sleep Apnea

Sleep apnea is a serious sleeping disorder. It occurs when patients stop breathing while they're sleeping. Sleep interruptions may occur infrequently or hundreds of times per night, which causes the brain to receive insufficient amounts of oxygen. Sleep apnea occurs in one of two manifestations. The airway becomes blocked during sleep when patients have obstructive sleep apnea (OSA). Central sleep apnea (CSA) is a disorder in which brain signals fail to control breathing while you sleep.

### *Snoring*

Sleep apnea patients often first complain of snoring—or more accurately, their partners complain of it. Most often, patients visit a doctor for professional advice after their sleep-deprived partner demands it. Constricted airways cause the patient to snore loudly, resulting in poor sleep quality for both the patient and their partner.

### *Periodically Choking or Gasping While Sleeping*

Not everyone who snores has sleep apnea. However, when someone snores and gasps for air throughout the night, it's a sign that they have sleep apnea. The combination of snoring, gasping, and choking is the body's response to a struggle for oxygen. This may happen once per night or hundreds of times per night.

### *Inability to Fall Asleep or Remain Asleep*

Insomnia, which is the inability to fall asleep, usually exists alongside other issues. Those issues may be emotional issues, such as anxiety or depression, or physical issues, such as sleep apnea. A leading theory suggests that sleep apnea causes insomnia, because the person knows his/her breathing stops during the night, which causes a high level of anxiety. It's difficult to fall asleep when the mind is anxious and can't settle down. When a sleep apnea patient can fall asleep, they often find it difficult to remain asleep. That person may be woken up by the sound of her own snoring/gasping. That person may also wake up because the brain is alerting them that something is wrong.

### Disturbed Sleep

Sleep apnea patients find it nearly impossible to get a good night's sleep. A high-quality night's sleep consists of alternating cycles of REM and non-REM sleep. Sleep apnea prevents the body from properly cycling back and forth between these two. As a result, sleep quality degrades drastically, leaving the patient feeling unrested and fatigued.

### Frequently Waking Up with a Sore Throat

Sleep apnea patients often wake up with a dry or a sore throat. This is because their mouths are open during most of the night. Sleeping with one's mouth open causes the throat's mucous membranes to dry out. This leads to an uncomfortable or painful feeling in the throat that may last all day.

### Weight Gain

Poor quality sleep can also result in weight gain. When we don't get enough high-quality sleep, our bodies produce an excessive amount of a hormone called ghrelin. Ghrelin tells our bodies that they need to eat. A lack of sleep also causes our bodies to produce less of a hormone called leptin. This is what signals our bodies to stop eating. Sleep may also affect insulin levels. Sleep deprivation makes our bodies insulin-resistant, which causes additional insulin production. The body will crave unhealthy foods.

### Feeling Sleepy Throughout the Day

Many factors of sleep apnea contribute to poor sleep quality. When the patient experiences all these symptoms, it affects their day-to-day life. They may find themselves waking up feeling as though they haven't slept. Patients may also be unable to complete simple tasks without fatigue and weakness dragging them down.

## Forgetfulness

Sleep apnea patients often find themselves becoming increasingly forgetful or scatterbrained. Children with sleep apnea are particularly susceptible to this symptom. It may decrease their ability to learn in school and may cause hyperactive or angry behavior. As a result, misdiagnosis of ADHD or other behavioural disorders may occur.

## Mood Swings

Depression, irritability, or anxiety may occur as a result of sleep deprivation. This may be related to sleep apnea, insomnia, or other sleep disorders. The chronic fatigue that sleep apnea patients often experience can develop into full-blown depression. Irritability, anxiety, and impatience are also common symptoms, because the mind is unable to focus on everyday tasks. An inability to focus initially leads to feelings of frustration. This often later morphs into short, but powerful, bouts of irritability and impatience.

## Lack of Interest in Sex

Testosterone, the hormone associated with sex drive in both men and women, increases when we sleep. If testosterone levels do not rise appropriately, then their libido decreases. A lack of testosterone can result in erectile dysfunction in men. Women may experience issues like decreased sexual sensation and desire as a result of inadequate testosterone.

# Restless Legs Syndrome (RLS)

Restless Legs Syndrome is a type of sleep-movement disorder. Restless legs syndrome, also called Willis-Ekbom disease, causes an uncomfortable sensation and an urge to move the legs while you try to fall asleep. Research indicates that there is a direct relationship between magnesium intake and sleep disturbances, insomnia, and restless legs syndrome (RLS). Essentially, magnesium inhibits excitatory NMDA receptor activity in the brain, and promotes GABA-A receptor activity—a process that stimulates relaxation, which in turn allows one to fall asleep.

The physiological causes of sleep disturbances and anxiety are similar. A double-blind clinical trial of older adults with insomnia found that 500 mg of magnesium per day, given as an oral supplement, significantly increased sleep time and sleep efficiency. It also significantly decreased insomnia severity scores and sleep onset latency (length of time needed to fall asleep), among other advantageous benefits. In terms of restless legs syndrome, how magnesium improves this condition is not understood at all; however, supplementation with 300 mg of magnesium daily was shown to significantly decrease periodic limb movements and improve sleep efficacy and overall sleep quality for those suffering with mild to moderate RLS caused by insomnia.

## Narcolepsy

Narcolepsy is a chronic neurological sleeping disorder that affects the brain's ability to regulate sleep-wake cycles. Patients that suffer from narcolepsy feel rested after waking up but may experience excessive daytime sleepiness, hallucinations, cataplexy, and sleep paralysis. Patients may also find themselves intermittently falling asleep uncontrollably throughout the day. Typically, people enter Rapid Eye Movement (REM) sleep within ninety minutes; however, people who suffer from narcolepsy fall into REM sleep almost immediately into their sleep cycle, as well as periodically throughout the day.

Narcolepsy is usually diagnosed between the ages of fifteen and twenty-five, but can be developed at any age. Narcolepsy affects approximately one in every two thousand Americans and about three million people worldwide. However, the condition is frequently misdiagnosed or undiagnosed, often going untreated. In a recent study, sixty percent of patients were misdiagnosed, with the most common misdiagnoses being depression, insomnia, and obstructive sleep apnea. It is estimated that only 25 percent of patients who have narcolepsy have been diagnosed and are receiving treatment. The average time from the onset of the symptoms to the diagnosis of narcolepsy is seven years.

Excessive Daytime Sleepiness (EDS) is one of the most common symptoms of sleep-deprived disorders, including narcolepsy. Approximately twenty percent of the population is affected by it. Those who have EDS feel sluggish and drowsy most days, which can impact their productiveness at work, school, activities, hobbies, or relationships. Another symptom of EDS is an increased pressure to fall asleep throughout the day, which can be life-threatening when operating a vehicle or heavy machinery. Most patients are treated with positive-pressure devices. However, some other treatments such as medications, dental appliances, and surgery work on a case-to-case basis. It is best to consult a psychiatrist before attempting to treat EDS or narcolepsy. (Janes, 2016)

## Symptoms of Sleep Problems

Symptoms of sleep disorders include being very sleepy during the daytime and having trouble falling asleep at night. Other symptoms are breathing in an unusual pattern or feeling an uncomfortable urge to move while you sleep.

## Story Share by Harley
## Sleep Deprivation to the Life-Saving PAP Device

*My name is Harley, and this is a true story. In fact, it is my personal journey into years of suffering, pain, and anguish owing to an undiagnosed condition called obstructive sleep apnea. Many years of incorrect diagnosis and treatment by several well-meaning doctors prevented me from getting the proper treatment for my condition. I tell my story in the hope that physicians and other health workers will recognize the urgency of their learning about sleep apnea and prescribing testing for this most under-diagnosed condition. I hope as well that people with the symptoms of sleep apnea will take this condition very seriously. It could save lives, possibly yours.*

*My story concerning sleep apnea is rather long. At first, I wanted to give long, detailed information going back to the 1980s, or even before that, in the military in the 1970s. There are so many heart episodes throughout these years that I will* only highlight some of them for you. I thought it prudent to begin at an event in August 1991, an event that changed everything about my life, and for the next ten years almost ended it.

From 1989 to 1993, I was a radio host of a live-talk program on radio station KKLA in Los Angeles, CA. My program was from midnight to two a.m. Monday through Friday. I enjoyed my work, and it was some of the greatest times in my life on radio.

My wife was with me that evening. After the program, we were driving home to Santa Ana, a bit more than an hour from the studio. About five miles from the house, I felt my heart began to beat uncontrollably, both in the rhythm and speed. Since I was driving, I was very concerned that I might be having a heart attack or stroke. This was the first time that something this serious had happened to me, and I immediately awakened my wife and told her of my condition and that I was going to the hospital. We went to Fountain Valley Regional Hospital. There I was seen by the on-call physician. By then it was 3:30 in the morning. In those years, my normal pulse was probably seventy beats per minute.. At the hospital that morning, it was over 150. I spent the next day there before I was transferred to Kaiser Permanente. I spent the next two days there. The main objective was to get the heart rate down to normal, which my caregivers managed to do late in the evening of the first day. I was kept overnight for observation. I asked the doctor what the reason for my condition was. His answer was surprising. He said that he had no idea what caused it. This answer would be repeated for the next nine years!

I was referred to a specialist two days later, and they ran an electrocardiogram and sent me away with medication. Since they did not know the cause, this began the journey of many disappointing "treatments" of different medications. I was prescribed a drug called atenolol. Atenolol is called a "beta blocker." Beta blockers are drugs that lower blood pressure by reducing the amount of blood pumped by the heart. This treatment brought about fatigue, nausea, drowsiness, and dizziness. I was taken off this medication after two days. What is interesting about this "treatment" was that none of the doctors ever told me what was wrong. Every one of them said that they could not pinpoint what was wrong, but that they would treat me for what they thought the problem could be.

What they did not tell me was that atenolol is given for those who have had a heart attack! Certainly, I didn't have a heart attack. This medication was replaced

## CHAPTER 8: SLEEP PROBLEMS

by one called, verapamil, which is a calcium or channel blocker. Calcium blockers relax blood vessel walls, thereby lowering blood pressure. I was on verapamil for about a year. It was more tolerable than atenolol, but I stopped taking it because of the side effects. It also did not maintain a reasonable blood pressure.

From 1991 until 2001, my life began to nosedive. I began to suffer off and on from massive headaches, usually in the summer, but not exclusively. These headaches lasted up to two weeks and no treatment would stop them. I was prescribed Tylenol with codeine, as well as extra strength over-the-counter medications. None of them worked. I was also having horrible nightmares, but until I began CPAP treatment many years later, I had no thought that the nightmares and sleep apnea were related.

As the headaches increased, so did the heart episodes. In 1995, again stricken while driving, I was taken to the same Fountain Valley Hospital, and again spent three days there and heard the same conclusion from the doctor: He could not tell me exactly what the cause of the heart problem was. This time, though, different medications were prescribed. I was put on Toprol, another beta blocker, along with Zestril. Toprol is given to patients who have had mild heart failure. Zestril is one of the newer medications called angiotensin-converting enzyme inhibitors. ACE inhibitors expand blood vessels and decrease resistance. This allows blood to flow more easily and makes the heart work easier. Zestril is prescribed for patients with congestive heart failure. Keep in mind that no doctor has ever told me the direct cause my heart suffering. Heart episodes continued, from one doctor to another with the same conclusion, urging me to take stronger doses of the medicine.

July 1999 saw one of the most traumatic episodes to date. My wife again rushed me to Fountain Valley Hospital and the on-call doctor, who this time inverted me and injected me with nitroglycerine. It was the most frightening and excruciating pain and fear that I have ever experienced. My rapid heart rate dropped so fast that I was disoriented. My hands and legs were flailing, and I had no control over my body. My hearing was gone, and I was on the verge of vomiting and passing out. All of this was done to force the heart back to a regular rhythm. Two days after that, I was sent home; not only with the same drugs I was already taking but with nitroglycerine tablets.

In 2000, I wanted off the Topril, because it made me sick. I was also prescribed hydrochlorothiazide, a diuretic. Zestril, or lisinopril, is now the only medication that I am taking.

*I had been told that I had cardiac arrhythmias (irregular heartbeat), atrial fibrillation, etc., but no firm diagnosis was offered as to the cause of any of these alleged conditions. Not only that but a heart ultrasound performed in July 1999 showed no heart abnormalities. I had been treated for heart disease, but there was never a connection between the cause and cure.*

*During all this time, I was increasingly irritable, fatigued, gaining weight, losing the ability to concentrate, lethargic, sickly, and the list goes on. I could never get enough sleep and never get to sleep! I took two naps some days and still never felt rested. It was at this time that I progressed to the worst state of my life, with all these symptoms climaxing in October 2001. That was the day I was subjected to electrical cardioversion to reset my heart rhythm. An intravenous anesthetic was injected, and patches were placed on my chest. After I was completely anesthetized, a small electrical charge was delivered over the heart. The charge caused a momentary electrical discharge of all the cardiac cells and allowed the primary pacemaker to take control of the rhythm, thus stopping the atrial fibrillation and resetting the heart.*

*This was it. I had no more solutions. The emergency room doctor told me that unless I lost weight I was going to die. I told my wife that I feared the next time I would be in a hospital concerning my heart I would have a heart attack or stroke. I was resolved to face the fact that I was probably going to die.*

*In November 2000, I met (again) Alex. Currently, he was working at St. John's Medical Center. He had been prodding me to come to a "sleep study." I had no idea what he was talking about and thought the entire matter of sleep being the cause of my issues was foolishness. I told him that all I needed to do was to lose weight and I would be just fine.*

*In December 2001, he prodded me again with the idea that I might have the disease called "sleep apnea." Frustrated, cranky, overmedicated, and with a blistering headache, I went to St. John's to prove to Alex that his studies concerning me were all wrong. On New Year's Eve 2001, swerving all over the 405 freeway, I finally got to St. John's, and there he explained to me exactly what sleep apnea was, and I began to get more curious as he explained to me that my life was characteristic of someone with sleep apnea. He wired me up, prepared the bed and CPAP machine, and away I went to sleep.*

*When I woke up on New Year's Day 2002, it was a rude awakening. The study showed that during sleep, my oxygen levels steadily decreased from a percentage in the high 90s to the low 70s. That was serious. Not only that, but he showed me how many times I stopped breathing! It was quite a shock. The very first words from my mouth after I saw the results was, "Hook me up!"*

*The result of using the CPAP machine was nothing short of astonishing! The next day, I had tremendous energy! I also noticed that I slept throughout the night. The position that I lay down in bed was the same position I was in when I rose from sleep. I noticed immediately that I had no more headaches, no more fatigue, no more snoring, no more nightmares, no more sleepless nights, and no more heart episodes! The proper treatment corrected all the horrific symptoms that had plagued my life for many years. From the day of my delivery from this ill-health bondage, I have been telling people I know, especially those who have similar symptoms that I had, to get tested. I know that for me, the proper diagnosis of my medical condition literally saved my life. I now can fulfill one of my lifelong desires; weight training and cardio. My exercise program has never been better. I am training better at fifty years old than I did in my twenties! Whenever I speak of Alex, I always refer to him as "the man God used to save my life."*

## Story Share by Anonymous
## Diagnosed with Insomnia Disorder

*Gary, a forty-year-old tradesman, saw a doctor to discuss his problems staying asleep. The trouble began four months prior, when he started to wake up at three a.m. every morning, no matter when he went to bed, and he was unable to fall back to sleep. As a result, he felt "out of it" during the day. This led him to feel more worried about how he was going to finish his projects when he was unable to focus due to extreme fatigue. At first, he did not recall waking up with any concern on his mind. As the problem lasted, he found himself dreading the next day and wondering how he would teach his apprentices or focus on his paperwork if he was only getting a few hours of sleep. Some mornings, he lay awake in the dark next to his fiancée, who was sleeping soundly. On other mornings, he would cut his losses, rise from bed, and go very early to his office.*

*After a month of poor sleep, Gary went to the local health services clinic, where he received his medical care. (He had asthma, for which he sometimes used an inhaler.) The physician assistant prescribed a sleep mediation, which did not help.*

*Falling asleep was never his problem, Gary explained. Meanwhile, he followed some of the advice he read online. Although he often relied on coffee during the day, he never drank it after two p.m. An avid swimmer, he chose to go in the early morning. He did have a glass or two of wine every night at dinner with his fiancée, however. "By dinner, I start to worry about whether I'll be able to sleep," he said, "and to be honest, the wine helps."*

*Gary did not appear tired but told the doctor, "I made a point to see you in the morning, before I hit the wall." He did not look sad or on edge and was not sure if he had ever felt depressed. But he was certain of nagging, low-level anxiety. "This sleep problem has taken over," he explained. "I'm stressed about my work, and my fiancée and I have been arguing. But it's all because I'm so tired."*

*Gary was diagnosed with insomnia disorder. His sleep problem began during a period of high stress. His worries about not sleeping may have made the problem worse. Gary may also have been self-medicating with caffeine to stay alert during the day and with wine to slow down during the evening.*

*Also noted is a past medical history of asthma, for which Gary sometimes uses an in haler. Because the inhaler mediation may be stimulating, knowing when and how much of them he uses would be helpful.*

# CHAPTER 9

## OBSESSIVE-COMPULSIVE DISORDER (OCD)

Obsessive-compulsive disorder is defined by constant thoughts and actions obsessing over violence, relationships, handwashing, and sexual actions, to name a few. The most common sign of OCD is excessive hand washing. Other obsessions can cause intrusive visuals, impulses, or even actions. This disorder is classically defined as the obsessive and inextinguishable need for control. However, misfiring in the brains of sufferers is also to blame. Misfiring leads to intrusive thoughts that are distressing and almost impossible to overcome, especially without medication. Obsessions about cleanliness and hygiene also cause extreme depression and anxiety. All these symptoms and signs can negatively affect the victims' lives and those around them.

OCD can be considered a difficult disorder to diagnose, because people can hide their symptoms for years. As a result, many refer to OCD as the secretive disorder. Individuals with this illness are often too skittish to explain their symptoms to a doctor, because they fear embarrassment. This can also lead to excessive counting, organizing, and cleaning. People who think they may have this disorder may end up harming themselves. This is often done inadvertently. The individual's hands may become injured due to over washing. Their anxiety and depression skyrockets. This leads to an uptick in self-harm and suicides. The preceding reasons are an explanation of the disorder, but also examples of how important it is to speak to your physician. If you feel like you may be suffering from OCD, make an appointment now to avoid further pain in the future.

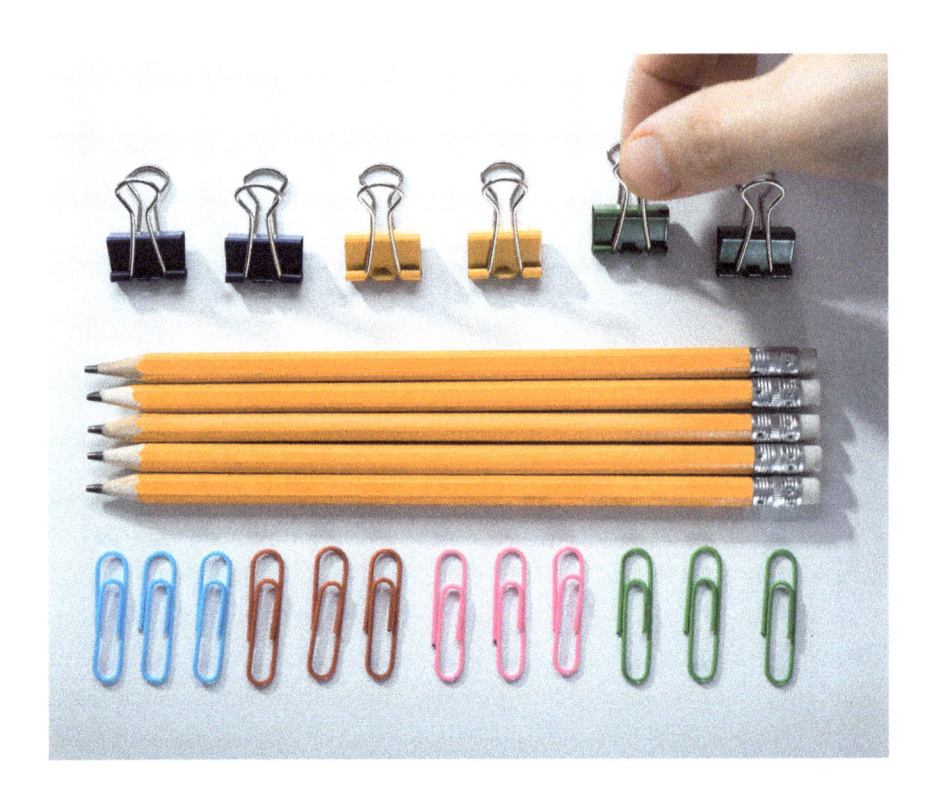

## Excessive Hand Washing

Excessive hand washing is the most observed symptom of OCD. It makes the sufferers feel more in control of their lives. The amount of time they wash their hands and how often they do so will help decide if the action is indeed compulsive. A normal amount of time to spend washing your hands is anywhere from twenty to sixty seconds. If you spend more time than that, it could be considered a compulsive behaviour. Additionally, excessive pressure and scrubbing aren't needed. Compulsive hand washers tend to wash their hands multiple times a day. They do not wash them for normal reasons either. There are usual activities that require hand washing. They include meal prep, bathroom use, after meals, changing diapers, blowing your nose, sneezing, coughing, taking out the garbage, touching animals, and disposing of animal waste. Washing for reasons beyond ones like these are considered obsessive. The problem may become severe enough to cause redness, swelling, bleeding, and splitting of the hands. Sufferers are split into two sections. The first includes individuals who are afraid of contamination beyond levels that most people feel. The second is composed of people that are afraid of contaminating others. Compulsive cleanliness is a common behaviour of people with OCD and their hands are no exception.

## Overzealous Cleaning

For victims of obsessive-compulsive disorder, obsessing over cleanliness may seriously interfere with their quality of life. Keeping your house clean and organized is normal. However, once it reaches the level that affects your family or friends, it can be considered obsessive. A usual amount of cleaning can amount to an hour or so each day, or a few hours of catch-up housework during the weekends. On the flip side, spending multiple hours stressfully cleaning each day is a sign of OCD. They may continuously check each room to make sure it is spotless. This checking behaviour spreads to many areas of the person's life.

## Checking Behaviour

Checking behaviour is a major sign of OCD. People with this disorder will check things like locks, burners, and important documents. They check these things over and over until they feel secure. People with OCD feel threatened by the world. Their fear is exaggerated to the extent that they agonize over it until it calms. Usually, they won't feel relief until they're convinced to stop the checking behaviour. Sometimes, sufferers will check things that seem less important to a normal state of mind. These include checking if the television, toaster, coffee maker, or lights are off. This compulsive behaviour is one of many. Another serious symptom of obsessive-compulsive disorder is counting things extensively.

## Counting

Obsessive counting is a common symptom of OCD. This symptom may or may not present itself. Counting compulsions include counting things over and over. Another symptom will cause them to perform tasks a special number of sequences. Some numbers may even have extra importance to the person. Individuals with OCD will count sidewalk sections, train cars, grapes, and whatever else they feel the need to. Their counting disorder stems from inappropriate fears. The fears they feel seem real to them. Some people do understand the irrationality of their fears. However, awareness of this often isn't enough to make them stop. Counting things is a form of over-organization. This is another symptom.

## Organization

Staying organized is a normal part of everyday life. In contrast, OCD often presents itself in an individual as an obsession with organization. The sufferer will fear loss, judgment, and chaos. Consequently, they will overly organize each day. They feel the need to control every situation they are in. Their homes are no exception. The association with control and cleanliness lead to this obsession. Symmetry is another form of this symptom. Oftentimes, the individuals will organize items, so they are in complete symmetry and alignment. An example of this would be straightening the top of a work desk. Papers, pens, staplers, and other items could seem in utter chaos to the sufferer. They will take extra time to straighten each item until they feel secure again. Insecurity and fear are extremely prevalent in OCD patients. They will range from severe to debilitating fears.

## Fears of Violence

One of the worst fears associated with OCD is an irrational fear or obsession with violence. People with this disorder can have intrusive thoughts about being harmed or inflicting violence upon others. These fears of violence can cause graphic thoughts that cause emotional distress and get in the way of leading a normal life. Everyone has violent thoughts from time to time. In fact, almost eighty-five percent of people admit to having these thoughts. The difference is that people with OCD cannot often rid themselves of these terrible thoughts. These are caused by a misfiring of the brain. They do not reflect on a person's values or moral code. They are simply intrusive thoughts. Other versions of these thoughts can make their way into the brains of sufferers as well.

## Unwanted Sexual Thoughts

Unwanted sexual thoughts that repeat are often signs of OCD. Mostly, they are unwanted and extreme. As a result, people with this symptom can feel extremely depressed and shameful. Feeling ashamed of these thoughts is the number one reason people seem to avoid treatment. They're afraid of being judged, or they may be in denial of their problem. Obsessive sexual thoughts tend to focus on acts with animals, children, or indecent exposure. Individuals will have visions of themselves performing terrible or inappropriate sexual behaviours. They may also have constant doubt about their true sexual identity. Some feel that they could eventually act on these intrusive thoughts. Subsequently, this leads to more anxiety. They will dwell on these thoughts until they go crazy. Relationships are another subject they might dwell on excessively.

## Dwelling on Relationships

People will always think about their relationships. Doing this is most productive. However, it isn't productive to dwell on them. This is another sign of

OCD. There are ways to discern the difference between the two. Everyone feels uncertain at some point in their relationship, but sufferers cannot deal with uncertainty. Obsessive thoughts can take a toll. People with OCD will obsess over whether they are making the right decision to be with their loved one, and they cannot handle the fact that they could make the wrong decision. They will also dwell on their relationship and whether their partner is loyal or not. These signs will cause their need for reassurance to grow.

## Seeking Reassurance

Seeking reassurance is another sign of OCD. Now, it isn't uncommon to need reassurance occasionally. However, sufferers of this disorder will always need it. They feel insecure and fear loss. Therefore, loved ones will constantly be required to reassure the person of their love and devotion. This is especially true when they're experiencing feelings of uncertainty. Family and friends can feel stressed out by this. The individual will also need reassurance in other areas. Their fears may cause them to need reassurances with other symptoms like intrusive thoughts, fears of violence, and compulsive cleanliness. This common sign of OCD will be helped by the supporting family and friends to not always reassure the sufferer. The less the subject is obsessed with reassurance the better. (Healthy Info Daily, 2019)

## Story Share by Anonymous
## OCD and Me

*My battle with obsessive-compulsive disorder started out like so many others. The earliest symptoms I can remember appeared around age eight. I had started to develop a prayer routine at night, which in my OCD mind, I believed would keep my loved ones safe. I felt I had to say my family member's names eight times, touch the right side of the wall after, blink eight times after that, and the list goes on. With so many rules and restrictions, I could not complete the prayer "perfectly" no matter how hard I tried. I vividly remember, it was late at night and my mom was still up cleaning. I ran down to her and burst into tears, because I could not get my prayers right and was so worried that my loved ones would be hurt because of this. This was the early nineties and my parents had no knowledge of OCD. My mom brushed this off as a silly childhood quirk and was not at all alarmed that something more serious might be happening.*

*Obsessions and compulsions continued on and off throughout my childhood and changed themes but usually fixated on my health and a fear of dying from AIDS, cancer, leukemia, appendicitis, a brain tumour, etc. My OCD was more just background noise while I was young but became stronger when I was getting ready to leave for college. For me, it seems that anytime I have a major transition in my life, which involves a large change, my OCD comes on full force. I have had two major episodes; one being going to college and the other being a relocation my husband and I made from the state for his job.*

*With my first episode, I had heard bits and pieces here and there about OCD and figured I had it, but so badly wanted to believe I did not. I compulsively asked my parents over and over whether I had OCD, and if I was going crazy. Since I functioned fine and was a successful high school student, they assured me that everything was fine with me and that I did not have OCD. I even insisted on an appointment with my then pediatrician, who was uneducated on OCD and as well assured me that I was fine. Once I got to college, the stress leveled out, and I was doing very well again.*

*My second and by far most destructive episode came seven years later. At this point, I had completely forgotten about OCD and thought it was just some quirk and phase I went through when I was younger. A lot of stress happened to me in the span of a year: a breakup and makeup with my now husband, my grandma passed away, I got engaged, was looking at a possible relocation, and trying to figure out a career. At some point, this all came to a head and my long, lost friend OCD came back with a vengeance.*

*Like all sufferers, this was a horrible time of anxiety for me that lasted a while. I lost a ton of weight, had a very hard time sleeping, could not concentrate on work, and was constantly seeking reassurance and barely functioning.*

*My testimonial for Beyond OCD is a long time coming, because I thought that in order to share my story, I had to have complete victory over OCD. The biggest lesson I have learned over the last year, and that Susan really helped me to accept, is that OCD is a disorder that I need to accept as part of my life for the long haul and continue to manage. For the periods of time when I am feeling well, and stress is low, I do just fine. When stress is higher, I have my struggles but have learned to manage much better. I recently came off medication, as my husband and I would like to start a family soon and have just begun therapy again, so that I can stay on top of my OCD. I hope my story gives others hope, as you can live a completely happy and fulfilling life even with OCD. I am living proof.*

## Story Share by Carla
## An Obsession with Potholes

*I was in my early twenties and having obsessive thoughts. I couldn't figure out why they were happening or what was going on. I had a couple of different ones that rotated. One was that I was going to fall asleep while driving. Another was that I was going to drop my car keys in a sewage hole. Another was that I was going to drop my keys in the crack between the elevator doors. Another one was that, every time I hit a pothole, I thought I had accidentally run someone over with my car.*

*I started to fear the thoughts so much that I would avoid doing things that I normally did. I would have other people drive, or drive around potholes... Do you know how many potholes are on the road these days? A lot.*

*I did some Google searching and matched how I was feeling with OCD. Then I just knew. What had been going on for months had a name and other people experienced it as well. I was not functioning at the level that I should have been.*

*I was diagnosed by a psychologist, and at first, saw her often for treatment. I only see her as needed now. In addition to cognitive behavioural therapy strategies, I try to live a healthy life. I don't smoke, drink (<u>alcohol</u> or <u>caffeine</u>), or do drugs. I go to the gym a couple days per week and take a lot of walks around a large lake nearby. If I'm having obsessive thoughts, I tell myself that they are nothing to fear.*

# CHAPTER 10

## ANGER

**A**nger or **wrath** is an intense emotional state. It involves a strong uncomfortable and hostile response to a perceived provocation, hurt, or threat.

A person experiencing anger will often experience physical conditions, such as increased heart rate, elevated blood pressure, and increased levels of adrenaline and noradrenaline. Some view anger as an emotion that triggers part of the fight or flight brain response. Anger is used as a protective mechanism to cover up fear, hurt, or sadness. Anger becomes the predominant feeling behaviourally, cognitively, and physiologically when a person makes the conscious choice to act to immediately stop the threatening behaviour of another outside force. The English term originally comes from the term *anger* of Old Norse language.

Anger can have many physical and mental consequences. The external expression of anger can be found in facial expressions, body language, physiological responses, and at times public acts of aggression. Facial expressions can range from inward angling of the eyebrows to a full frown. While most of those who experience anger explain its arousal as a result of "what has happened to them," psychologists point out that an angry person can very well be mistaken because anger causes a loss in self-monitoring capacity and objective observability.

Modern psychologists view anger as a primary, natural, and mature emotion experienced by virtually all humans at times, and as something that has functional value for survival. Uncontrolled anger can, however, negatively affect personal or social well-being and impact negatively on those around them. While many philosophers and writers have warned against the spontaneous and uncontrolled fits of anger, there has been disagreement over the intrinsic value of anger. The issue of dealing with anger has been written about since the times of the earliest philosophers, but modern psychologists, in contrast to earlier writers, have also pointed out the possible harmful effects of suppressing anger.

CHAPTER 10: ANGER

## What Is Anger?

Everyone knows the feeling. It's that rage that rises when a driver is cut off on the highway and he just wants to floor it and flip the bird. Anger is a corrosive emotion that can run off with a person's mental and physical health. Is holding it in the solution? Or letting it all out? Anger doesn't dissipate just because it is unleashed; in fact, that just rehearses it. However raw it can be, anger is a necessary emotion, serves mankind well in certain situations, and like all emotions, benefits from good management lest it cause self-harm or erupt into hostile, aggressive, or perhaps even violent behaviour toward others.

Anger is considered one of the basic emotions, along with happiness, sadness, anxiety, and disgust. Researchers posit that these emotions have served a protective purpose over the long course of human history. Anger is related to the "fight, flight, or freeze" response of the sympathetic nervous system; it prepares human faculties for the first option: to fight. But fighting doesn't necessarily mean throwing punches; it might motivate communities to combat injustice by changing laws or intentionally shifting norms of behaviour. Of course, anger too easily or frequently mobilized can undermine relationships, and studies show, it is deleterious to bodies in the long term. Prolonged release of the stress hormones that accompany anger can destroy neurons in areas of the brain associated with judgment and short-term memory, and it can weaken the immune system. (Phycology Today, 2019).

## Why Are Some People Angrier Than Others?

According to Jerry Deffenbacher, PhD, a psychologist who specializes in anger management, some people really are more "hotheaded" than others; they get angry more easily and more intensely than the average person does. There are also those who don't show their anger in loud spectacular ways but are chronically irritable and grumpy. Easily angered people don't always curse and throw things; sometimes they withdraw socially, sulk, or get physically ill.

People who are easily angered generally have what some psychologists call a low tolerance for frustration, meaning simply that they feel that they should not have to be subjected to frustration, inconvenience, or annoyance. They can't take things in stride, and they're particularly infuriated if the situation seems somehow unjust: for example, being corrected for a minor mistake.

What makes these people this way? Several things.

One cause may be genetic or physiological: There is evidence that some children are born irritable, touchy, and easily angered, and that these signs are present from a very early age. Another may be sociocultural. Anger is often regarded as negative; we're taught that it's all right to express anxiety, depression, or other emotions but not to express anger. As a result, we don't learn how to handle it or channel it constructively.

Research has also found that family background plays a role. Typically, people who are easily angered come from families that are disruptive, chaotic, and not skilled at emotional communications (American Psychological Association, 2019).

## Story Share by Anonymous
## Soft Answers Remove Anger. Rough Words Raise Rage.

*I read this short, interesting story online, and I would like to share it as the answer to the question. Probably many already know this one. It goes like this:*

*One night a snake, while it was looking for food, entered a carpenter's workshop.*

*The carpenter, who was a rather untidy man, had left several of his tools lying on the floor.*

*One of them was a saw. As it went around inside the shop, the snake climbed over the saw, which gave it a little cut.*

*At once, thinking that the saw was attacking it, the snake turned around and bit it so hard that its mouth started to bleed, enraging the snake even more. The snake continued to attack the saw repeatedly until the saw was covered with the snake's blood. Sadly, the snake did not realize what was happening.*

*Dying from its own wounds, the snake decided to wrap itself around the saw and began to squeeze with all its strength, but alas! It ended up killing itself.*

*Sometimes during certain life situations, we react with anger, not realizing that we are only hurting ourselves. In life, it's better to sometimes ignore situations,*

## CHAPTER 10: ANGER

*people, and their behaviour. People say and do things, but it's our decision whether to react in a positive or in a negative way.*

*The carpenter and his tools in this story are like those unpolished, insensitive people and their equally insensitive utterances that cut us in the heart, hurt our sentiments, and cause us emotional damage. But it is up to us to either ignore them and go our way without letting their words touch/harm us or to react foolishly like the snake in this story and end up in a miserable condition due to our short temper.*

"*Soft answers remove anger. Rough words raise rage.*"

## Story Share by Anonymous
## Anger and Love

*While a man was polishing his new car, his six-year-old son picked up a stone and scratched lines on the side of the car. In anger, the man took the child's hand and hit it many times, not realizing he was using a wrench.*

*At the hospital, the child lost all his fingers due to multiple fractures. When the child saw his father, with painful eyes, he asked, "Dad, when will my fingers grow back?" The man was so hurt and speechless; he went back to his car and kicked it a lot of times. Devastated by his own action, sitting in front of that car, he looked at the scratches; the child had written,*

*"LOVE YOU DAD."*

*Anger and Love have no limits; choose the latter to have a beautiful, lovely life. Things are to be used and people are to be loved. But the problem in today's world is that people are used, and things are love. Let's be careful to keep this thought in mind: Things are to be used, but people are to be loved.*

*Watch your thoughts; they become words. Watch your words; they become actions. Watch your actions; they become habits. Watch your habits; they become character. Watch your character; it becomes your destiny.*

## Story Share by Anonymous
## Trying to Fix it Myself

*John knew his anger was a problem and kept trying to fix it himself. He searched the internet for anger management success stories but didn't get help until it was nearly too late.*

*When John lost it in front of his wife and sons again, he knew this time he'd crossed the line. Looking back, he doesn't know why he threw the saltshaker at the oven in front of the whole family. It just happened.*

*Afterwards, he realized that his reaction was overblown, as well as being hurtful to his wife and children. He hated the intense guilt he had after a blow-up. He apologized to everyone in his family, but he could tell that they were uneasy around him. He also hated that this family was afraid of him.*

*John's wife, Linda, had been asking him for a long time to get control of his anger. He thought he could do it by sheer will or by counting to ten, as so many websites advised him to do. Nothing worked. Nothing he tried could turn him into one of the anger-management success stories he wanted to become. So, he turned to counselling, John immediately felt comfortable sharing and discovered his triggers. He learned five tools he could use to stop his anger from getting out of control. He also found out where his anger came from and began to manage those sources. John's family is much more relaxed around him now, and he no longer must feel such intense guilt.*

# CHAPTER 11

# SELF-ESTEEM

What is self-esteem? Self-esteem means feeling good about yourself.

**People with self-esteem:**
- feel liked and accepted
- are proud of what they do
- believe in themselves

**People with low self-esteem:**
- feel bad about themselves
- are hard on themselves
- think they are not good enough

## Where Does Self-Esteem Come From?

Parents, teachers, and others. The people in our lives can affect how we feel about ourselves. When they focus on what's good about us, we feel good about ourselves. When they are patient when we make mistakes, we learn to accept ourselves. When we have friends and get along, we feel liked.

But if adults scold more than they praise, it's hard to feel good about yourself. Bullying and mean teasing by siblings or peers can hurt self-esteem, too. Harsh words can stick and become part of how you think about yourself. Luckily, it doesn't have to stay that way.

The voice in your own head and the things you say to yourself play a big part in how you feel about yourself. Thinking *I'm such a loser* or *I'll never make friends* hurts your self-esteem.

There are other ways to think about the same things: *I didn't win this time … but maybe next time* or *Maybe I can make some friends.* That voice is more hopeful. It helps you feel okay. And it could turn out to be true.

Sometimes, the voice in our head is based on harsh words others have said. Or on bad times we have faced. Sometimes, the voice is just us being hard on ourselves. But we can change the voice in our own head. We can learn to think better of ourselves. (Lyness, 2018)

Learning to do things. We feel good when we learn to read, add, draw, or build. Play a sport, play music, write an essay, ride a bike. Set the table, wash the car. Help a friend, walk the dog. Each thing you learn and do is a chance to feel good about yourself. Step back and look what you can do. Let yourself feel happy with it.

But sometimes we're too hard on ourselves. We don't accept that what we do is good enough. If we think, *It's not really any good,* or *It's not perfect,* or *I can't do it well enough*, we miss the chance to build self-esteem.

## What if My Self-Esteem is Low?

You can do things to feel better about yourself. It's never too late. Here are some tips to raise your self-esteem: Be with people who treat you well. Some people act in ways that tear you down. Others lift you up by what they say and do. Learn to tell the difference. Choose friends who help you feel okay about yourself. Find people you can be yourself with. Be that type of friend for others.

Say helpful things to yourself. Tune in to the voice in your head. Is it too critical? Are you too hard on yourself? For a few days, write down some of the things you say to yourself. Look over your list. Are these things you'd say to a good friend? If not, rewrite them in a way that's true, fair, and kind. Read your new phrases often. Do it until it's more of a habit to think that way.

Accept what's not perfect. It's always good to do the best you can. But when you think you need to be perfect; you can't feel good about anything less. Accept your best. Let yourself feel good about that. Ask for help if you can't get past a need to be perfect.

Set goals and work toward them. If you want to feel good about yourself, do things that are good for you. Maybe you want to eat a healthier diet, get more fit, or study better. Make a goal. Then plan for how to do it. Stick with your plan. Track your progress. Be proud of what you've done so far. Say to yourself, "I've been following my plan to work out every day for forty-five minutes. I feel good about it. I know I can keep it up."

Focus on what goes well. Are you so used to talking about problems that they're all you see? It's easy to get caught up in what's wrong. But unless you balance it with what's good, it just makes you feel bad. Next time, catch yourself when you complain about yourself or your day. Find something that went well instead.

Give and help. Giving is one of the best ways to build self-esteem. Tutor a classmate, help clean up your neighbourhood, walk for a good cause. Help at home or at school. Make it a habit to be kind and fair. Do things that make you proud of the kind of person you are. When you do things that make a difference (even a small one), your self-esteem will grow.

## What is Self-Esteem?

Confidence in one's value as a human being is a precious psychological resource and generally a highly positive factor in life; it is correlated with achievement, good relationships, and satisfaction. Possessing little self-regard can lead people to become depressed, to fall short of their potential, or to tolerate abusive situations and relationships. Too much self-love, on the other hand, results in an off-putting sense of entitlement and an inability to learn from failures. It can also be a sign of clinical narcissism, in which individuals may behave in a self-centred, arrogant, and manipulative manner. Perhaps no other self-help topic has spawned so much advice and so many (often conflicting) theories.

Self-esteem can influence life in myriad ways, from academic and professional success to relationships and mental health. Self-esteem, however, is not an immutable characteristic; successes or setbacks, both personal and professional, can fuel fluctuations in feelings of self-worth. Everyone's experience is different, but over the course of the lifespan, self-esteem seems to rise and fall

CHAPTER 11: SELF-ESTEEM

in predictable, systematic ways. Research suggests that self-esteem grows, by varying degrees, until age sixty, when it remains steady before beginning to decline in old age.

## How to Understand Self-Actualization

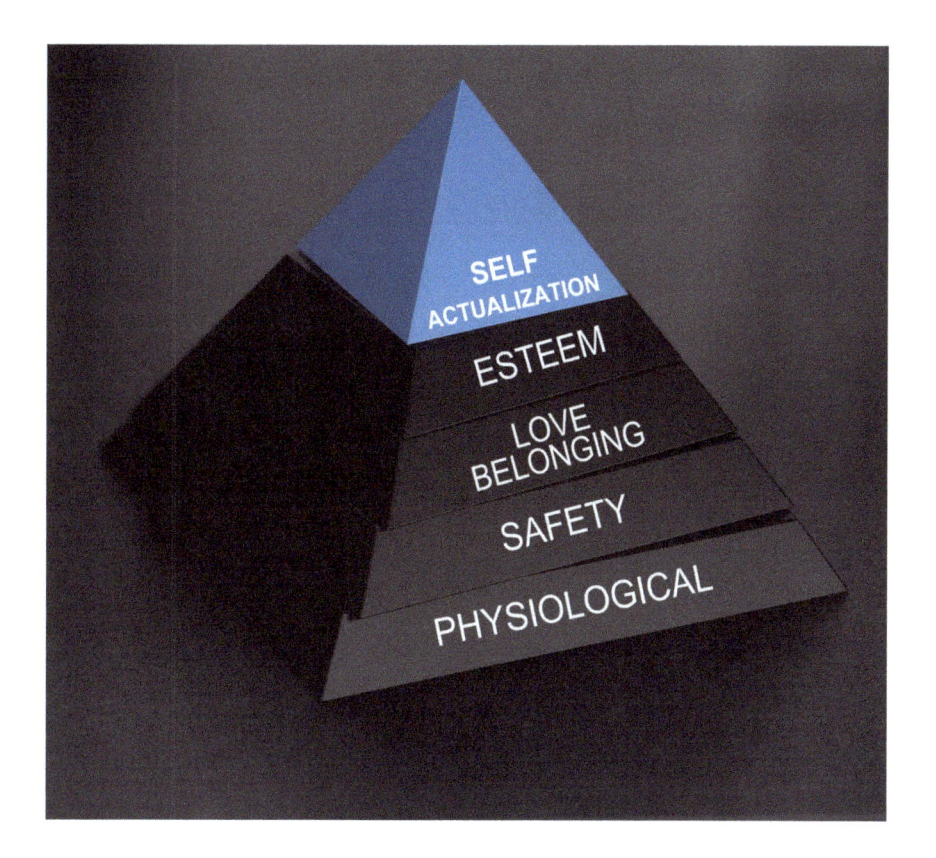

Self-actualization represents the pursuit of reaching one's full potential. The concept is rooted in a theory established in 1943 by Abraham Maslow. The psychologist set forth a hierarchy of psychological needs, illustrating an order of human motivation. At the base of Maslow's motivational pyramid lies physiological needs, such as the air we breathe and the food we consume. Once those needs are met, it is possible to pursue needs for safety, love and belonging, and self-esteem. Self-actualization occurs when the more basic needs are met or in the process of being met, and it becomes possible to strive to add meaning and personal and social fulfillment to existence through creativity, intellectual growth, and social progress. As Maslow himself stated, "What a man can be, he must be. This need we may call self-actualization.

## Story Share by Anonymous
## High School a Complete Wreck

*What was the main reason for your low self-esteem? My life during high school was a complete wreck. I was 5'9" and weighed over 230 pounds. As a result of being overweight, I always kept a low profile at school and was a very shy and quiet person, so that people would not comment on my appearance. Also having a face full of zits and gigantic glasses did not really help boost my self-esteem. On one occasion, I was even humiliated in high school for liking a boy who was thin. I had told my friends in confidence that I liked a certain boy, and my friends told his friend who in return laughed at me in front of my friend, and suggested that their friend didn't like fat girls. Although I laughed it off and denied that I liked him, I remember thinking to myself how I could not wait to get home and cry my heart out. After this experience and spending such a long time tormenting myself over my excess weight, I decided that it was time to lose the weight, only it was after high school. Nevertheless, I lost fifty pounds, and it boosted my self-esteem, but not as much as I expected.*

*You see, I always thought that thin people had incredible self-esteem, but what I forgot to think through is that I was overweight in my mind, and that the shy girl afraid of anyone calling her ugly or making a negative comment on her weight was still very much alive in my mind. What I am trying to achieve by sharing my story is to advise people that may have a weight problem and have low self-esteem that, in order for us to be happy, we should not only aim to work on ourselves externally, but try to shape our interior as well: such as our way of thinking. <u>Ourselves</u>.*

*What have you done to raise your self-esteem? I have learned to speak openly about my weight. Now I can stare at a person who may call me fat and tell them that my appearance is none of their concern. I have learned to appreciate every compliment any person gives me, and when I feel down, I look in a mirror at myself and repeat the latest compliment I have received. Exercise has also helped me relieve stress and increase my self-esteem, because I feel like I am doing something great for my health.*

*What self-esteem-boosting advice would you offer others? I feel that if any person has tried exercises to raise self-esteem and end up feeling worse, do not hesitate and seek counseling. It is extremely helpful to speak to a person that listens to you and someone you feel you can trust.*

## Story Share by Anonymous
## I was Bullied at School

*Guess I was perhaps born with it too, but it probably kicked in at school and got worse at secondary school. I wasn't beautiful, funny, smart, or sporty so where do you fit in? Nowhere. I was bullied at school, more mental than physical, just catty girl stuff, rejected by boys. I suffered awful depression during my teens, hated myself, and this has been the general pattern even to now. I have had relationships, which have been too much to handle, with people who had addictions and I would try to fix them, and in the end, made myself unwell, with a bit of a breakdown.*

*This is how I feel when relationships end, and I generally believe I will be on my own forever and it will never work out for me, which makes me so sad. I'm going to be the only one of four children from my family to be unmarried, no children, and it hurts to think like this—like I have no real future or plans or anything that makes me positive or happy about my future. I've maybe gotten a bit better looking, but deep down, don't have confidence or truly feel that I deserve to be loved by a partner.*

*What have you done to raise your self-esteem? I have tried to speak to friends, but you know how busy people can be, and I feel that I'm a bit of a broken record. I do try to remember compliments, but negatives always outweigh my positives in my head. I also had a bit of CBT, which did help. I just wished I could keep my counsellor forever, but I fear I might always feel like this. I have for at least the last fifteen to twenty years.*

*What self-esteem-boosting advice would you offer others?* Wished I could take my own advice. If you find inner strength, walk on and walk tall. Try to think of a moment where, inside, you felt a swell of pride in yourself on a job well done, getting a job etc., and try to focus on good times.

*What would you like to share about your background, who you are?* I am from an African background.

*What was the main reason for your low self-esteem (or that of a friend)?* I made a resolution from my infancy that I will remain a virgin till I am married. However, a senior male friend whom I respected made me sleep with him after keeping that promise up till age twenty-four, and so I felt I had lost my self-worth, I was no good, and cannot stand by my decisions. I could no longer stand where issues of virginity are discussed, even though I am married now and above forty.

*What have you done to raise your self-esteem?* I tried to see it as past now, and should not allow past events to weigh me down.

*What self-esteem-boosting advice would you offer others?* Seek superior advice on issues you cannot handle, because that was my problem. I suspected the moves, but didn't know the steps to take to avert them, and that was why I became a victim.

# CHAPTER 12
## SUICIDAL FEELINGS

Suicide—when someone intentionally takes their own life—is a very complex issue. You're not alone; many of us have had suicidal thoughts at some point in our lives. Feeling suicidal is not a character defect, and it doesn't mean that you are crazy, or weak, or flawed. It only means that you have more pain than you can cope with right now. This pain seems overwhelming and permanent now. But with time and support, you can overcome your problems, and the pain and suicidal feelings will pass.

## Be the Kind of Person

―――――

Be the kind of person to ask someone if they are okay, twice if they say they are, but look like they are not.

Be the kind of person who smiles at people even if they don't smile back.

Be the kind of person you wished for when no one was there for you.

Be the kind of person who is brave enough to stand alone in a crowd for what is right.

Be that person, because we need more people like that in the world.

Be that person, because people like that are rarer than the rarest diamonds and gold.

Nikita Gill

CHAPTER 12: SUICIDAL FEELINGS

## Having Suicidal Thoughts

No matter how much pain you're experiencing right now, you're not alone. Some of the finest, most admired, needed, and talented people have been where you are now. Many of us have thought about taking our own lives when we've felt overwhelmed by depression and devoid of all hope. But the pain of depression can be treated, and hope can be renewed. No matter what your situation, there are people who need you, places where you can make a difference, and experiences that can remind you that life is worth living. It takes real courage to face death and step back from the brink. You can use that courage to face life, to learn coping skills for overcoming depression, and for finding the strength to keep going. Remember:

- Your emotions are not fixed. They are constantly changing. How you feel today may not be the same as how you felt yesterday, or how you'll feel tomorrow or next week.

- Your absence would create grief and anguish in the lives of friends and loved ones.
- There are many things you can still accomplish in your life.
- There are sights, sounds, and experiences in life that have the ability to delight and lift you, and that you would miss.
- Your ability to experience pleasurable emotions is equal to your ability to experience distressing emotions.

NATIONAL SUICIDE PREVENTION LIFELINE

We can all help prevent suicide. The Lifeline provides 24/7, free and confidential support for people in distress, prevention and crisis resources for you or your loved ones, and best practices for professionals.

**tel:1-800-273-8255**

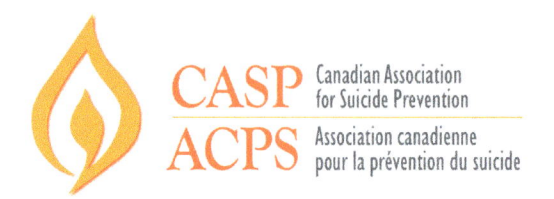

| | | |
|---|---|---|
| Centre de prévention du Suicide d'Abitibi-Ouest | www.cpsao.org | 819-339-3356 |
| Valley View Funeral Home | www.valleyviewsurrey.ca | 604-596-8866 |
| Toronto Distress Centre | www.torontodistresscentre.com | 416-408-HELP (4357) |

| | | |
|---|---|---|
| Safe Haven Women's Shelter Society | www.tabersafehaven.ca | 403-223-0483 |
| Centre Prévention Suicide Faubourg | www.cpsfaubourg.org | 1-866-APPELLE (277-3553) |
| CMHA British Columbia - Vernon | http://vernon.cmha.bc.ca | 1-888-353-2273 |
| Telephone Aid Line Kingston | www.telephoneaidlinekingston.com | 613-544-1771 |
| Capital Region Mental Health & Addictions | www.crmhaa.ca | |
| NEED2 | www.need2.ca | |
| HEARTBEAT | http://heartbeatsurvivorsaftersuicide.org/20170826_v481/about-heartbeat-2/ | |
| Centre Prévention Suicide d'Amos | www.preventionsuicideamos.org | |
| Centre de prévention du suicide | www.preventionsuicide.ca | 1-866-APPELLE (277-3553) |

| | | |
|---|---|---|
| Prairie Mountain Health | www.prairiemountainhealth.ca | Crisis Services: over the age of 18 - North: 1-866-332-3030; South: 1-888-379-7699; under the age of 18 - North: 1-866-332-3030; all areas: 1-866-403-5459 |
| Distress Centre of Ottawa & Region | www.dcottawa.on.ca | 613-238-3311 |
| Centre de prévention du suicide Côte-Nord | www.preventionsuicidecotenord.ca | 1-866-APPELLE (277-3553) |
| La maison sous les arbres | www.la-msla.com | 450-699-5935 |
| Vancouver Island Crisis Society | www.vicrisis.ca | 1-888-494-3888 |
| Vancouver Island Crisis Society | https://www.vicrisis.ca/ | 1-888-494-3888 |
| Le Tournant | www.letournant.org | 450 371-4090 |
| Distress Centre of Lanark, Leeds and Greville | https://developmentalservices.com/ | 1-800-465-4442 |
| BC Bereavement Helpline | www.bcbh.ca | 1-877-779-2223 |

| | | |
|---|---|---|
| Centre de prévention suicide de la Haute-Yamaska (Granby et région) | www.cpshy.qc.ca | 450-375-4252 |
| Wheatland Crisis Society | www.strathmoreshelter.com | (403) 934-6634 or 1-877-934-6634 |
| Centre de prévention du suicide de Lanaudière | https://cps-lanaudiere.org/ | 1-866-APPELLE (277-3553) / 450 759-6116 |
| North East Outreach and Support Services | http://northeastoutreach.ca/ | 1.800.611.6349 |
| Fraser Health Crisis Line A program of Options Community Services | https://www.options.bc.ca/program/fraser-health-crisis-line | 604.951.8855 \| 1.877.820.7444 |
| Crisis Line Association of BC | https://www.crisislines.bc.ca/ | 1-800-784-2433 / 310-6789 |
| Canadian Mental Health Association – Edmonton Region | www.edmonton.cmha.ca | 780-482-HELP (4357) |
| Canadian Mental Health Association for the Kootenays | www.kootenays.cmha.bc.ca | Crisis Line)1-888-353-2273 (Mental Health Line) 310-6789 or 1-800 suicide (1-800-784-2433) |

| | | |
|---|---|---|
| Kamloops Suicide Loss Support Group | http://fb.me/suicide-losssupportgroup | |
| BC Bereavement Helpline | www.bcbh.ca | 604-738-9950 or 1-877-779-2223 |
| Telecare Crisis & Caring Line | www.telecarebc.com | 1-888-852-9099/ Tollfree, 604-852-9099 Abbotsford/Mission |
| Chimo Helpline | http://www.chimo-helpline.ca/ | 1-800-667-5005 & 1-506-450-HELP (4357) |
| Distress Centre Durham | www.distresscentre-durham.com | 905-430-2522 OR 1-800-452-0688 |
| CMHA/PEI | www.pei.cmha.ca | 902-628-3669 |
| Distress Centre Calgary | https://www.distress-centre.com/ | 403.266.4357 |
| Craigwood Youth Services | www.craigwood.ca | 519-433-0334 |
| Distress Centre Niagara | www.distresscentreniagara.com | St. Catharines, Niagara Falls & Area 905-688-3711, Port Colborne, Welland, Wainfleet & Area 905-734-1212, Fort Erie & Area 905-382-0689, Grimsby, West Lincoln & Area 905-563-6674 |

|  |  |  |
|---|---|---|
| Huron Hospice | www.huronhospice.ca | (519) 482-3440 Ext. 6300 |
| Dr. Margaret Savage Crisis Centre | https://dmscc.ca/ | 780-594-3353 or 1-866-594-0533 |
| Trans Lifeline | www.translifeline.org | 877-330-6366 |
| Nunavut Kamatsiaqtut Help Line | www.nunavuthelpline.ca | 613-601-5082 |
| JEVI Centre de prévention du suicide – Estrie | www.jevi.qc.ca | 819 564-1354 |
| Lethbridge Family Services | www.lfsfamily.ca | |
| Some Other Solutions | https://someothersolutions.ca/ | 780-743-4357 |
| CMHA Calgary | www.cmha.calgary.ab.ca | |
| Government of the NWT | https://www.hss.gov.nt.ca/en | 1-800-661-0844 |
| Prince Albert Mobile Crisis Unit | www.pacrisis.ca | 306-764-1011 |

| | | |
|---|---|---|
| **Canadian Mental Health Association Alberta Southeast** | http://cmha-aser.ca/ | |
| **Wood's Homes** | https://www.wood-shomes.ca/programs/community-resource-team/ | 1-800-563-6106 |

## What Are Suicidal Feelings?

People feel suicidal for a variety of reasons, for example:

- Life has become too difficult or hopeless because of external events like a relationship break-up or the symptoms of a mental-health problem.
- They are experiencing intrusive thoughts about suicide or hearing voices that instruct them to take their own life.

The risk of someone acting to end their life can be made worse by heightened feelings of carelessness or impulsivity. This might be caused by symptoms of a mental-health problem, such as mania, or if they have been consuming drink or drugs.

It is difficult to know how common suicidal feelings are, as many people describe them in different ways, and many will never ask for support. However, a recent survey estimated that around 20 percent of the population will experience suicidal feelings in their lifetime and 6.7 percent of people will act to end their lives.

## Myths and Misconceptions About Suicidal Feelings

Suicide and suicidal feelings can be hard to talk about, because some people think they are a sign of weakness or being selfish. This can then lead to people hiding how they feel when they need help, and puts lives at risk. (Time to Change, 2019).

One common misconception is that someone with suicidal feelings **will** act to end their life

If someone is experiencing suicidal thoughts or feelings, it does not always mean they intend to act on them. People feel suicidal for a variety of reasons:

- They may be experiencing intrusive thoughts or hearing voices (hallucinations), which do not reflect how they feel.
- They may be experiencing a very low mood, which they are resisting and know will pass.
- There is a myth that, because someone asks for help or shares their feelings about wanting to end their life, they are not serious about acting on their feelings. Some people think a suicide attempt is a 'cry for help' and not a genuine intention to end their life. This is both an inaccurate and uncaring description:
- Many people who take actions to end their lives want to die, even if they survive and come to a different perspective later.
- Even for those who would like someone to intervene, if someone is so desperate that they are willing to risk their lives, they need attention and compassion, not judgment and dismissal.

## Is Suicide Selfish?

Some people criticize the person who has died by suicide for not considering the feelings of friends and family, or even strangers who are disrupted if the act has taken place in public. There is in fact a strong argument to say that suggesting someone who is suffering so extremely that they want to die should put the needs of others ahead of their own is the selfish attitude.

People who are feeling suicidal are in no position to consider the needs of others, because their distress is so great. Some also describe feeling strongly that their loved ones would be better off without them.

People who have survived suicide attempts describe excruciating pain before, during, and afterwards. It is in no way easy or painless.

Suicidal feelings can be something that someone experiences once, or they might be something that they have to deal with on and off their whole lives. Suicidal thoughts can take over someone's life, prevent them from maintaining relationships, doing their jobs, or looking after their physical health. It is extremely stressful and frightening to consider death for long periods of time, with no hope of relief. Going about your day-to-day life when you feel life is not worth living is also exhausting.

## How Can I Help Someone with Suicidal Feelings?

Be direct. Talking about suicide is not easy, even for those of us who do not believe it is shameful and want to be compassionate. This means we sometimes use euphemisms or talk around the topic instead of approaching it directly. If you are concerned someone is thinking of ending their life, ask them honestly whether they feel unsafe and whether they have a specific plan.

Not only will it help you find out how best to support them, but by being direct you will be taking away some of the shame and secrecy around suicidal feelings, which can also reduce their impact.

Everyone's experience of suicidal feelings is unique to them. You might feel unable to cope with the enduring difficult feelings you are experiencing. You may feel less like you want to die and more like you cannot go on living the life you have.

These feelings may build over time or might fluctuate from moment to moment. And it's common to not understand why you feel this way.

Suicidal feelings can be overwhelming. How long these feelings last differs for everyone. It is common to feel as if you'll never be happy or hopeful again. But with support and self-help, most people who have felt suicidal go on to live fulfilling lives. The earlier you let someone know how you're feeling, the quicker you'll be able to get support to overcome these feelings.

However, it can feel difficult to open up to people.

You may want others to understand what you're going through, but you might feel:

- unable to tell someone
- unsure of who to tell
- concerned that they won't understand
- fearful of being judged
- worried you'll upset them

## How Can I Cope Right Now?

### Distract Yourself

If you're thinking of harming yourself, **find self-harm coping techniques that work for you:**

- hold an ice cube in your hand until it melts and focus on how cold it feels
- tear something up into hundreds of pieces
- take a very cold shower or bath. See the tips for coping with self-harm.
- **Focus on your senses.** Taking time to think about what you can smell, taste, touch, hear, and see can help to ground your thoughts.
- **Steady your breathing.** Take long deep breaths; breathing out for longer than you breathe in can help you to feel calmer.
- **Look after your needs.** Avoid taking drugs or drinking alcohol, as this can make you feel worse. If you can, get a glass of water, eat something if you're hungry, sit somewhere comfortable, and write down how you're feeling.
- **Get outside.** If you are feeling numb, feeling the rain, sun, or wind against your skin can help you to feel more connected to your body.

- **Reach out.** If you can't talk to someone you know, contact a telephone support service or use online peer support.

Even if your suicidal thoughts and feelings have subsided, get help for yourself. Experiencing that sort of emotional pain is itself a traumatizing experience. Finding a support group or therapist can be very helpful in decreasing the chances that you will feel suicidal again in the future. You can get help and referrals from your doctor or from the organizations listed in the above chapter.

## Five Steps to Recovery

**Identify triggers or situations** that lead to feelings of despair or generate suicidal thoughts, such as an anniversary of a loss, alcohol, or stress from relationships. Find ways to avoid these places, people, or situations.

**Take care of yourself.** Eat right, don't skip meals, and get plenty of sleep. Exercise is also key, as it releases endorphins, relieves stress, and promotes emotional well-being.

**Build your support network.** Surround yourself with positive influences and people who make you feel good about yourself. The more you're invested in other people and your community, the more you must lose, which will help you stay positive and on the recovery track.

**Develop new activities and interests.** Find new hobbies, volunteer activities, or work that gives you a sense of meaning and purpose. When you're doing things you find fulfilling, you'll feel better about yourself and feelings of despair are less likely to return.

**Learn to deal with stress in a healthy way.** Find healthy ways to keep your stress levels in check, including exercising, meditating, using sensory strategies to relax, practicing simple breathing exercises, and challenging self-defeating thoughts (Jaffe et al. 2018)

# CHAPTER 12: SUICIDAL FEELINGS

## Story Share by Anonymous
## Suicide is not the Answer

*Before I became suicidal, my life was, in a word, "a mess." I come from a truly dysfunctional family, in which I suffered what at first appeared to be episodes of depression. I was hospitalized on three occasions during my late teen years and therefore managed only to graduate from grade twelve (grade thirteen was incomplete). When I was nineteen, I was raped on the "first date" I had. In my family, dating was not an option until marriage was on the horizon.*

*From this disastrous beginning, I met my first husband, and I would have married him even he had had three heads and an extra eye in the middle of his forehead. My misfortune was that he was abusive, and so I finally got rid of him after five years.*

*Shortly thereafter, I met my second (and present) husband and the three of us (including my son from my first marriage) moved to London to start life over. When I got pregnant again, I sent my son to stay with my parents, as my husband was attending school and I thought a short stay would be all right. However, after the birth of my daughter, my parents refused to give me back my little boy.*

*It was at this point that I became suicidal. I left the hospital alone and went back to my apartment. I could not comprehend a life without my little boy, and I truly believed that they would side with my first husband no matter what. I just could not stand thinking about my life anymore, and so I decided to kill myself by jumping off the balcony. We were five stories high and the basement made it six stories. At the very last second, as I hung onto the railing of the balcony, I did not want to die, but it was too late. I landed on the parking-lot pavement.*

*When I came to, I saw a lot of bodies dressed in white. I remember saying, "Where is God?" Somebody replied, "She's alive!" I remember swearing, because I had thought that God could fix the misery I felt.*

*If someone should think that ending their life is a good solution, I can attest to the fact that it is not. The pain that I felt was indescribable. I had a broken leg (above and below the knee), broken pelvis, broken arm, and so on. They could not set any bones until I was stabilized. The doctors inserted a steel pin just above my knee and put my leg in traction. People who try to kill themselves and fail are privy to a mess they can in no way imagine. The physical pain can be unbearable. Then you get to see the pain and horror in the eyes of someone you love and who* loves you. Many people suggested to my husband that he should leave me in the hospital, go on with life, and forget about me.

During the process of recovery in the hospital, my husband was with me every day.

When I was released from the hospital, my husband tried his best to encourage me to walk again. And with the help of psychiatrists and a later hospitalization, I was diagnosed as bipolar. Since 1983, I have been taking lithium and have never had a recurrence of suicidal thoughts or for that matter any kind of depression.

A few years later, I began a business in my home. Eventually my husband and I moved to a commercial address, and he worked for the business as well. Daily contact with customers gave me the self-assurance I lacked. When I was able to assist them in finding and securing good employment opportunities, they told me that I was "wonderful" and that I had been responsible for their success. I helped a lot of people who thought I was great, and soon I started to share their assessment of me. My work also enabled me to learn a lot about people and to empathize with their job successes and failures. In other words, I became a friend.

I truly believe that, if a person is suicidal, that person does not feel any self-worth. Such a person also probably feels inadequate and unable to resolve issues that for them are truly heartbreaking.

The first reason for me to go on living was seeing the love my husband had for me, even though I had been so self-destructive and essentially had abandoned him. The second reason was that, though I did not have my son, I had a daughter who also loved me and needed me. I see my first son often now, which is very important to me. Thirdly, my customers gave me purpose and validation. Why go on living when the world is sometimes a very hurtful place and it seems that "you just can't win?" As I now like to say, "Everything shall pass one day ... even the good stuff." Nothing stays the same, and therefore, one never knows what changes may come.

The oddest thing in the whole world has been for me to recognize that no one looks at you and judges you as to your social and economic status. Having an open mind and being willing to listen has made it possible for me to establish relationships with individuals from all walks of life.

In short, suicide is not the answer. It is only the accumulation of bad feelings that can change. Life can be good if you wait.

CHAPTER 12: SUICIDAL FEELINGS

## Story Share by Anonymous
## We Are More Powerful Then We Know

*Yesterday, I listened to the presentation on this project at the Canadian Association for Suicide Prevention Conference in Dartmouth and realized why I was there, besides trying to learn basic knowledge to save someone else's life.*

*My story of my suicide attempt isn't typical, in the fact that it ended differently, maybe because I was meant to fight this cause today.*

*I'm the fifth generation of mental illness in my family. Some families have diabetes, others have heart problems, but for me, everyone had mental-health issues. I'm from a small, isolated community in far Northern Ontario, where mental health is very taboo even today. So, as you can imagine, I was raised in a very dysfunctional environment. By age five, I had been emotionally, physically, and sexually abused. By age six, I had a baby sister and I was forgotten. I was quiet, shy, and usually scared. The only time they remembered I existed was to scream at me or use me to release their anger. By age nine, I was the victim of my teacher's bullying. She would humiliate me in front of the class, and then I would go home to WWIII. I hated my existence.*

*By age eleven, everything was falling apart. My mother and stepfather hated each other and fought in very violent ways in front of us. Six months later, my stepfather just left, and no one knew where he had disappeared to. The same night, there was a new man in the house. Even more violent. He was the main drug dealer in my town, and he would beat my mother all the time. She would then turn her anger on me, so by the age of twelve, I had enough. Even the responsibility of raising my little sister wasn't enough to convince me to stay alive.*

*One summer night in July, at around midnight, I was very agitated and emotionally drained. I was walking frantically around the house, planning on how to release myself from this pain. I had learned from my mother's new boyfriend's ten-year-old daughter that taking lots of pills could set you free. So, I was ready—scared, but ready. I was going through our picture box to find a nice picture of me and my sister so I could let her know that I loved her, when I found a letter.*

*It was the letter my grandmother wrote before she shot herself in a dump, because she thought she was garbage. All I could think in my hysterical crying was how much life would have been different if she had been able to hold on. I couldn't give to my sister the pain I felt for my grandmother's death. So, I prayed to her to help me through this and made her a promise that I would fight the battle she had lost. A battle I have fought for seventeen years now. It was a horrible but rewarding path I had to take, but I'm here, and I know right now that tomorrow is a better day. Those twenty-nine years of knowledge saved my life and can save someone else's. That sometimes you have nothing tangible to hold on to, but a tiny sparkle of hope in your back pocket. Today, I am proud to be other people's sparkle of hope, and I feel blessed that I can relate to their stories no matter how hard. I've learned that life isn't and will never be hopeless. No matter how dark and terrifying a moment can become, we are all more powerful then we know.*

https://psychcentral.com/quizzes/depquiz.htm Maybe you have depression, take this quick quiz to see.

https://psychcentral.com/disorders/depression/ The specific symptoms of a full-blown episode of clinical depression.

https://www.metanoia.org/suicide/stigma.htm Prevents suicidal people from recovering. We are not only fighting our own pain but the pain that others inflict on us, and that we ourselves add to the stigma, which is a huge complicating factor in suicidal feelings.

https://www.metanoia.org/suicide/grief.htm Has anyone significant in your life recently died? Would you be in good company? Many suicidal people have recently suffered a loss.

https://www.metanoia.org/suicide/ptsd.htm While most suicidal people recover and go on, others struggle with suicidal thoughts and feelings for months or even years, and post-traumatic stress disorder (PTSD). (Metonia, 2018)

# CHAPTER 12: SUICIDAL FEELINGS

## Story Share by Corky
## I was a Soldier Once

*I liked the idea that, as the commercial said, we did more by 0700 than most people did all day. I loved, as range safety officer, getting shots down range by 0800. I loved the brutality of route marches, because they set us apart from my civilian friends, as most of them could never have hacked the pace. I liked standing in a United Nations observation post just before dawn in a faraway land, realizing that I and other soldiers in my unit were doing something very special by representing Canada and the Canadian people, undergoing physical and mental strains that many could not or would not face to keep our country safe and ready. I loved climbing up cargo nets in full battle order and repelling down cliffs. I loved running the assault course. I liked the early morning runs and the late-night polishing before a parade.*

*I liked the smell of the quartermaster stores, an odd mixture of gun oil, canvas preservative, leather, hemp rope, and cigarette smoke. I liked the racks of rifles and submachine guns, and I loved the gun sheds and tank hangers, where the vehicles and weapons of war gleamed dully and exuded strength and capability, and the power to "git 'er done," if need be.*

*I loved the name of the equipment when I started off, Sherman, Fabrique Nationale, Sten and Bren, because they spoke to me of the proud days when our fathers used them successfully in WWII. Our #36 Grenade was the same as our grandfathers used in WWI for God's sake! I also loved when the 105 mm and the M 109 gave way to the M 777, and the guns could shoot accurately over thirty kilometers. I loved it when the old lady "the deuce and a half" was finally replaced by the modern MLVW. The Centurion tank gave way to the Leopard, and within weeks, our tankers showed NATO they were the best.*

*I liked our soldiers, from all parts of the land, from cities of Upper Canada, small towns of Nova Scotia and Newfoundland. They came from the mountains and from the prairies, from all walks of life. I trusted and depended on them, as they trusted and depended on me for professional competence, for comradeship, for strength, and for courage. In a word, we were "soldiers," then and forever. I liked the surge in my heart when word was passed that a unit was deploying, and I loved the infectious thrill of riding homeward in convoy, waving at the cars we passed and at pedestrians who I was sure looked at us with envy as we rolled through their villages on our way back to base. I loved waving from the back of a truck at the kids in cars that would trail us for a while before finally passing.*

*The work was hard and dangerous, the going rough at times, and the parting from family painful, but the companionship of robust army laughter, and the "all for one and one for all" philosophy of the military, was ever present. I once enjoyed the best two hours sleep in my life laying on the ground at a rest halt while doing a patrol. The weather was overcast but warm and a slight drizzle did not deter my snoring, which could be heard four men down the line. Another four or five hours would have been nice, but there was work to be done.*

*I liked the fierce and dangerous activity of the Infantry Rifle Coy, as we began an advance to contact. I liked doing the recce for a harbor, where I had to hide up to forty pieces of wheeled and tracked equipment from the enemy. I hated having to run ahead of our vehicles in complete darkness and trying to be quiet as the drivers and co-drivers tried to back vehicles and trailers into a black hole as quickly as possible, so others in line could pass and find me and also be properly positioned and put away.*

*One could hear cursing and unmeant bitching as crews stumbled in the dark to erect cam nets and digging in for protection from an enemy attack. We cut and poked branches holding up the nets to break the vehicle outline so as not to be recognized. The lucky ones had a relatively small vehicle, and others a two and a half or a five ton. To cover that even in daylight would take an hour or more. At night it was dangerous, demanding, and extremely hard work. In the rain or freezing snow, this necessary chore was brutal.*

*Watching my fellow soldiers as they took down the cam nets, loaded fuel, ammunition, and rations for yet another long day, feeling truly exhausted and knowing it was going to get a lot worse before it got better, added value to the experience. We were soldiers, and this is what it was like.*

*I loved the name and the history of my regiments. I loved the parades, the colours on parade, and the Guidon presentation, the march past, the roll past, the advance in review order, and the sound of my hand slapping the stock of my rifle during the Present Arms. I could feel the National Anthem inside me while the band played it. Some liked "The Queen" or "O Canada." I loved "The Maple Leaf Forever."*

*I loved walking through our position in complete darkness, checking the welfare of my men and NCOs, and assuring them that they were not alone, as we stood in our trench at first light, on stand to. I liked the weight of my steel helmet on my head and the embrace of my webbing. It made you feel like Superman, though in your heart, you surely knew you were not. I loved the weight of my rifle or pistol and knowing I could outshoot a lot of my men. It was an ongoing competition during range practice to outdo your friends as well as your superiors.*

*There was pride in self and country, and growing mastery of the soldier's trade. An adolescent could find adulthood. A man could find fulfillment, and an old man finds great joy. I will never forget that I was once a soldier. There is no higher calling. I would do it again in a heartbeat. I liked the traditions of the army and those who made them.*

*I was a soldier once…*

# REFERENCES

Abuse, S., & Administration, M. H. S. (2016). 2015 National Survey on Drug Use and Health.

American Psychological Association. (2019) Why Are Some People Angrier Than Others? (Retrieved 18-04-2019) https://www.apa.org/topics/anger/control

Beck, A. T., Emery, G., & Greenberg, R. L. (2005). Anxiety Disorders and Phobias: A Cognitive Perspective. Basic Books.

Bisson, J. I., Roberts, N. P., Andrew, M., Cooper, R., & Lewis, C. (2013). Psychological Therapies for Chronic Post-Traumatic Stress Disorder (PTSD) In Adults. Cochrane Database of Systematic Reviews, (12).

Craske, M. G. (1999). Anxiety Disorders: Psychological Approaches to Theory and Treatment.
Boulder, CO: Westview Press.

Drugs, Brains, and Behavior: The Science of Addiction. (2018). (Retrieved 10-04-2019) https://www.drugabuse.gov/sites/default/files/soa_2014.pdf

Felman, A., (2018).What are the complications of Addictions, (Retrieved 24-03-2019) https://www.medicalnewstoday.com/articles/323461.php

Felman, A, (2018). "What is Addiction?" Medical News Today. MediLexicon, Intl. (Retrieved 10-04-2019) https://www.medicalnewstoday.com/articles/323465.php

Felman, A. (2018). "What is Addiction?" Medical News Today. (Retrieved 10-04-2019) https://www.medicalnewstoday.com/articles/323465.php

Figley, C. R. (2013). Compassion fatigue: Coping with secondary traumatic stress disorder in Those who treat the traumatized. Routledge.

Helping a family member or friend. (2015). (Retrieved 10-04-2019) https://www.ncadd.org/family-friends/there-is-help/helping-a-family-member-or-friend

Hoge, E. A., Ivkovic, A., & Fricchione, G. L. (2012). Generalized Anxiety Disorder: Diagnosis and Treatment. Bmj, 345, e7500.

Hoge, C. W., Riviere, L. A., Wilk, J. E., Herrell, R. K., & Weathers, F. W. (2014). The Prevalence of Post-Traumatic Stress Disorder (PTSD) in US combat soldiers: a head-to-head comparison of DSM-5 versus DSM-IV-TR symptom criteria with the PTSD checklist. The Lancet Psychiatry, 1(4), 269-277.

Jaffe, A. (2010). Alcohol, Benzos, and Opiates—withdrawal that might kill you. (Retrieved 10-04-2019) https://www.psychologytoday.com/us/blog/all-about-addiction/201001/alcohol-benzos-and-opiates-withdrawal-might-kill-you

Jaffee, J., Robinson, L., and Segal, J. (2018). Are you Feeling Suicidal? (Retrieved 23-04-2019) https://www.helpguide.org/articles/suicide-prevention/are-you-feeling-suicidal.htm

Janes, R. (2016). Understanding Narcolepsy; Symptoms, Causes and Treatment.

Gilbert, P. (2016). Depression: The evolution of powerlessness. Routledge.

# REFERENCES

Hawton, K., Witt, K. G., Salisbury, T. L. T., Arensman, E., Gunnell, D., Hazell, P., & van Heeringen, K. (2016). Psychosocial Interventions for Self-Harm in Adults. Cochrane Database of Systematic Reviews, (5).

Hom, M. A., Stanley, I. H., & Joiner Jr, T. E. (2015). Evaluating Factors and Interventions That Influence Help-Seeking and Mental Health Service Utilization among Suicidal Individuals: A Review of the Literature. Clinical psychology review, 40, 28-39.

Hysing, M., Stormark, K. M., & O'Connor, R. C. (2015). Sleep Problems and Self-Harm In Adolescence. The British Journal of Psychiatry, 207(4), 306-312.

Ibrahim, R. Z. A. R., & Ohtsuka, K. (2014). Review of the job Demand-Control and job Demand-Control-Support models: Elusive Moderating Predictor Effects and Cultural Implications. Southeast Asia Psychology Journal, 1.

Ivry, Sara (2002). Seasonal Depression can Accompany Summer Sun. The New York Times. (Retrieved 10-04-2019)

Kendall-Tackett, K. A. (2016). Depression In New Mothers: Causes, Consequences and Treatment Alternatives. Routledge.

Kim, J. J., La Porte, L. M., Saleh, M. P., Allweiss, S., Adams, M. G., Zhou, Y., & Silver, R. K. (2015). Suicide Risk among Perinatal Women Who Report Thoughts Of Self-Harm On Depression Screens. Obstetrics & Gynecology, 125(4), 885-893.

Lyness, D. (2018). Teens Health. How can I improve Self – Esteem?

MacDonald, L. (2019). "10 Lifestyle Methods to Cope with Seasonal Affective Disorder" (Retrieved 12-03-2019) https://www.activebeat.com/diet-nutrition/10-lifestyle-methods-to-cope-with-seasonal-affective_disorder/

Mayo Clinic (2018). Season Affective Disorder. (Retrieved 12-03-2019) https://www.mayoclinic.org/diseases-conditions/seasonal-affective-disorder/symptoms-causes/syc-20364651

Mayo Clinic (2019). Sleep Disorders. (Retrieved 16-04-2019) https://www.mayoclinic.org/diseases-conditions/sleep-disorders/symptoms-causes/syc-20354018

Metonia (2018). Suicide; Read this First (Retrieved 23-04-2019) https://www.metanoia.org/suicide/original.htm

Mond, J. M. (2014). Eating Disorders "Mental Health Literacy": An introduction.

O'Neil, A., Quirk, S. E., Housden, S., Brennan, S. L., Williams, L. J., Pasco, J. A., ... & Jacka, F. N. (2014). Relationship between Diet And Mental Health In Children And Adolescents: A Systematic Review. American journal of public health, 104(10), e31-e42.

Opiate overdose crisis. (2018). (Retrieved 10-04-2019) https://www.drugabuse.gov/drugs-abuse/opioids/opioid-overdose-crisis

Pantic, I. (2014). Online Social Networking and Mental Health. Cyberpsychology, Behavior, and Social Networking, 17(10), 652-657.

Roberts, C. (2019). 8 Different Types of Insomnia and Sleeplessness. https://www.activebeat.com/your-health/8-different-types-of-insomnia-and-sleeplessness/8/

Sauer, S. (2018). The 7 Stages of Dementia. Seniors Living Blog, The Caregivers guide to the 7 Stages of Dementia (Retrieved 14-04-2019)

# REFERENCES

Time to Change. (2019). Suicidal Feelings. (Retrieved 23-04-2019) https://www.time-to-change.org.uk/about-mental-health/types-problems/suicidal-feelings

Steenkamp, M. M., & Litz, B. T. (2013). Psychotherapy for Military-Related Posttraumatic Stress Disorder: Review of the evidence. Clinical psychology review, 33(1), 45-53.

Treatment. (2014). (Retrieved 10-04-2019) https://www.drugabuse.gov/related-topics/treatment

Trends & statistics. (2017). Drug Abuse (Retrieved 22-03-2019) https://www.drugabuse.gov/related-topics/trends-statistics

Trimble, M. R. (2013). Post-Traumatic Stress Disorder: History of A Concept. In Trauma And It's Wake (pp. 31-39). Routledge.

Penning, M. J., & Wu, Z. (2015). Caregiver Stress and Mental Health: Impact Of Caregiving Relationship And Gender. The Gerontologist, 56(6), 1102-1113.

Phycology Today, (2019). Anger. (Retrieved 22-03-2019) https://www.psychologytoday.com/ca/basics/anger

Rosenthal, N. E.; Sack, D. A.; Gillin, J. C.; Lewy, A. J.; Goodwin, F. K.; Davenport, Y.; Mueller, P. S.; Newsome, D. A.; Wehr, T. A. (1984). "Seasonal Affective Disorder. A Description of the Syndrome and Preliminary Findings with Light Therapy". Archives of General Psychiatry. 41 (1): 72–80.

Segal, Z. V., Williams, M., & Teasdale, J. (2018). Mindfulness-based cognitive therapy for depression. Guilford Publications

Signs and symptoms. (2016). (Retrieved 10-02-2019) https://www.ncadd.org/about-addiction/signs-and-symptoms/signs-and-symptoms

Vujanovic, A. A., Niles, B., Pietrefesa, A., Schmertz, S. K., & Potter, C. M. (2013). Mindfulness In The Treatment of Posttraumatic Stress Disorder Among Military Veterans.

Worden, J. W. (2018). Grief Counseling and Grief Therapy: A Handbook For The Mental Health Practitioner. Springer Publishing Company.

# WHY I WROTE THIS BOOK

I have been thinking about writing this book on mental health for quite a long time. It is to give you excellent strategies and coping mechanisms to understand the demons within, knowing that a high percentage of the population deal with them daily.

In my preparation for writing this book, I researched over thirty different types of mental illnesses. I have touched on almost half, and I hope you find a topic you can relate to, and it helps.

I truly believe that, once you get a glimpse of the big picture, you'll change the way you look at life and what it has to offer. Don't forget we are human, and it's okay to have a meltdown … only don't unpack and live there. Cry it out and then refocus on where you are headed.

Lastly, I wrote this book because I'm very passionate about the topic. If you've been told that you are broken, that your damaged goods and should be labeled a victim, I (for one) don't buy it. Truth be told, we are the men and women with the skills, determination, and values to ensure we mentor, coach, and instruct the next generation for their survival.

CPSIA information can be obtained
at www.ICGtesting.com
Printed in the USA
LVHW070055161119
637463LV00001B/1/P